Strength to Love

Martin Luther King was President of the Southern
Christian Leadership Conference and co-pastor
of Ebenezer Baptist Church, Atlanta, Georgia.
He led the dramatic 'walk for freedom' in
Montgomery, which resulted in bus desegregation,
and was active in the Albany movement. He
was chosen Man of the Year by *Time* Magazine
in January 1964. Dr King was assassinated on
April 4, 1968 in Memphis, Tennessee.

MARTIN LUTHER KING

Strength to Love

Collins
FOUNT PAPERBACKS

First printed in Great Britain by Hodder and Stoughton 1964
First issued in Fontana books 1969
Ninth Impression May 1976
Reprinted in Fount Paperbacks March 1977

© 1963 by Martin Luther King Jr.

Made and printed in Great Britain by
William Collins Sons & Co Ltd Glasgow

Contents

	Preface	page 7
I	A tough mind and a tender heart	9
II	Transformed nonconformist	17
III	On being a good neighbour	26
IV	Love in action	36
V	Loving your enemies	47
VI	A knock at midnight	56
VII	The man who was a fool	67
VIII	The death of evil upon the seashore	76
IX	Shattered dreams	86
X	How should a Christian view communism?	96
XI	Our God is able	106
XII	Antidotes for fear	115
XIII	The answer to a perplexing question	127
XIV	Paul's letter to American Christians	138
XV	Pilgrimage to nonviolence	147
	Sources	156

TO MY MOTHER AND FATHER
*whose deep commitment to the Christian faith
and unswerving devotion to its timeless
principles have given me an inspiring example
of the Strength to Love*

Preface

In these turbulent days of uncertainty the evils of war and of economic and racial injustice threaten the very survival of the human race. Indeed, we live in a day of grave crisis. The sermons in this volume have the present crisis as their background; and they have been selected for this volume because, in one way or another, they deal with the personal and collective problems that the crisis presents. In these sermons I have sought to bring the Christian message to bear on the social evils that cloud our day and the personal witness and discipline required. All of these sermons were originally written for my former parishioners in the Dexter Avenue Baptist Church of Montgomery, Alabama, and my present parishioners in the Ebenezer Baptist Church of Atlanta, Georgia. Many of the sermons were later preached to congregations throughout the nation.

All of these sermons were preached during or after the bus protest in Montgomery, Alabama, and I have drawn a number of illustrations from that particular movement, some of which were included in my book *Stride Toward Freedom*. Three of the sermons—"Love in action," "Loving your enemies," and "Shattered dreams"—were written while I was in Georgia jails. "Pilgrimage to nonviolence" is a revision and updating of material which previously appeared in *The Christian Century* and *Stride Toward Freedom*. Although it is not a sermon, it has been included at the end of the volume at the specific urging of the publisher.

I have been rather reluctant to have a volume of sermons printed. My misgivings have grown out of the fact that a sermon is not an essay to be read but a discourse to be heard. It should be a convincing appeal to a listening congregation. Therefore, a sermon is directed toward the listening ear rather than the reading eye. While I have tried to rewrite these sermons for the eye, I am convinced that this venture could never be entirely successful. So even as this volume goes to press I have not altogether overcome my misgivings. But in deference to my former congregation, my present congregation, my close associates in the Southern Christian Leadership Conference, and my many friends across the nation who have asked for copies of individual sermons, I offer these discourses in the hope that a message may come to life for readers of these printed words.

I am happy to express my deep gratitude to many helpers. I am indebted to my close friend and Executive Assistant, Wyatt Tee Walker, a fine preacher in his own right, for reading the entire manuscript and offering valuable suggestions. I am also indebted to my teacher and friend, Samuel W. Williams, for helpful and stimulating suggestions. Charles L. Wallis gave valuable editorial assistance on the final manuscript. My thanks also go to my efficient secretary, Miss Dora E. McDonald, who constantly offered encouraging words and transferred my handwritten pages to typewritten copy. Most of all I must thank my devoted wife Coretta, who has read the complete manuscript and given invaluable suggestions and inspiration. Her love and patience enabled her to be understanding in the face of my increased absence from her and our children while completing this volume.

MARTIN LUTHER KING

CHAPTER ONE

A tough mind and a tender heart

Be ye therefore wise as serpents, and
harmless as doves.   Matthew 10:16

A French philosopher said, "No man is strong unless he bears within his character antitheses strongly marked." The strong man holds in a living blend strongly marked opposites. Not ordinarily do men achieve this balance of opposites. The idealists are not usually realistic, and the realists are not usually idealistic. The militant are not generally known to be passive, nor the passive to be militant. Seldom are the humble self-assertive, or the self-assertive humble. But life at its best is a creative synthesis of opposites in fruitful harmony. The philosopher Hegel said that truth is found neither in the thesis nor the antithesis, but in an emergent synthesis which reconciles the two.

Jesus recognized the need for blending opposites. He knew that his disciples would face a difficult and hostile world, where they would confront the recalcitrance of political officials and the intransigence of the protectors of the old order. He knew that they would meet cold and arrogant men whose hearts had been hardened by the long winter of traditionalism. So he said to them, "Behold, I send you forth as sheep in the midst of wolves." And he gave them a formula for action: "Be ye therefore wise as serpents, and harmless as doves." It is pretty difficult to imagine a single person having, simultaneously, the characteristics of the serpent and the dove, but this is what Jesus expects. We must combine the toughness of the serpent and the softness of the dove, a tough mind and a tender heart.

I

Let us consider, first, the need for a tough mind, characterized by incisive thinking, realistic appraisal, and decisive judgment. The tough mind is sharp and penetrating, breaking through the crust of legends and myths and sifting the true from the false. The tough-minded individual is astute and discerning. He has a strong, austere quality that makes for firmness of purpose and solidity of commitment.

Who doubts that this toughness of mind is one of man's greatest needs? Rarely do we find men who willingly engage in hard, solid thinking. There is an almost universal quest for easy answers and half-baked solutions. Nothing pains some people more than having to think.

This prevalent tendency toward softmindedness is found in man's unbelievable gullibility. Take our attitude toward advertisements. We are so easily led to purchase a product because a television or radio advertisement pronounces it better than any other. Advertisers have long since learned that most people are softminded, and they capitalize on this susceptibility with skilful and effective slogans.

This undue gullibility is also seen in the tendency of many readers to accept the printed word of the press as final truth. Few people realize that even our authentic channels of information—the press, the platform, and in many instances the pulpit—do not give us objective and unbiased truth. Few people have the toughness of mind to judge critically and to discern the true from the false, the fact from the fiction. Our minds are constantly being invaded by legions of half-truths, prejudices, and false facts. One of the great needs of mankind is to be lifted above the morass of false propaganda.

Softminded individuals are prone to embrace all kinds of superstitions. Their minds are constantly invaded by irrational fears, which range from fear of Friday the thirteenth to fear of a black cat crossing one's path. As the elevator made its upward climb in one of the large hotels of New York City, I noticed for the first time that there was no thirteenth floor—floor fourteen followed floor twelve. On inquiring from the elevator operator the reason for this omission, he said, "This practice is followed by most large hotels because of the fear of numerous people to stay on a thirteenth floor." Then he added, "The real foolishness of the fear is to be found in the fact that the fourteenth floor is actually the thirteenth." Such fears leave the soft mind haggard by day and haunted by night.

The softminded man always fears change. He feels security in the status quo, and he has an almost morbid fear of the new. For him, the greatest pain is the pain of a new idea. An elderly segregationist in the South is reported to have said, "I have come to see now that desegregation is inevitable. But I pray God that it will not take place until after I die." The softminded person always wants to freeze the moment and hold life in the gripping yoke of sameness.

Softmindedness often invades religion. This is why religion has sometimes rejected new truth with a dogmatic passion. Through edicts and bulls, inquisitions and excommunications, the church has attempted to prorogue truth and place an impenetrable stone wall in the path of the truth-seeker. The historical-philological criticism of the Bible is considered by the softminded as blasphemous, and reason is often looked upon as the exercise of a corrupt faculty. Softminded persons have revised the Beatitudes to read, "Blessed are the pure in ignorance: for they shall see God."

This has also led to a widespread belief that there is a conflict between science and religion. But this is not true. There may be a conflict between softminded religionists and toughminded scientists, but not between science and religion. Their respective worlds are different and their methods are dissimilar. Science investigates; religion interprets. Science gives man knowledge which is power; religion gives man wisdom which is control. Science deals mainly with facts; religion deals mainly with values. The two are not rivals. They are complementary. Science keeps religion from sinking into the valley of crippling irrationalism and paralyzing obscurantism. Religion prevents science from falling into the marsh of obsolete materialism and moral nihilism.

We do not need to look far to detect the dangers of softmindedness. Dictators, capitalizing on softmindedness, have led men to acts of barbarity and terror that are unthinkable in civilized society. Adolf Hitler realized that softmindedness was so prevalent among his followers that he said, "I use emotion for the many and reserve reason for the few." In *Mein Kampf* he asserted:

> By means of shrewd lies, unremittingly repeated, it is possible to make people believe that heaven is hell—and hell, heaven. . . . The greater the lie, the more readily will it be believed.

Softmindedness is one of the basic causes of race prejudice. The toughminded person always examines the facts before he reaches conclusions; in short, he postjudges. The tenderminded person reaches a conclusion before he has examined the first fact; in short, he prejudges and is prejudiced. Race prejudice is based on groundless fears, suspicions, and misunderstandings. There are those who are sufficiently softminded to believe in the superiority of the white race and the inferiority of the Negro race in spite of the toughminded research of anthropologists who reveal the falsity of such a notion. There are softminded persons who argue that racial segregation should be perpetuated because Negroes lag behind in academic, health, and moral standards. They are not toughminded enough to realize that lagging standards are the result of segregation and discrimination. They do not recognize that it is rationally unsound and sociologically untenable to use the tragic effects of segregation as an argument for its continuation. Too many politicians in the South recognize this disease of softmindedness which engulfs their constituency. With insidious zeal, they make inflammatory statements and disseminate distortions and half-truths which arouse abnormal fears and morbid antipathies within the minds of uneducated and underprivileged whites, leaving them so confused that they are led to acts of meanness and violence which no normal person commits.

There is little hope for us until we become toughminded enough to break loose from the shackles of prejudice, half-truths, and downright ignorance. The shape of the world today does not permit us the luxury of softmindedness. A nation or a civilization that continues to produce soft-minded men purchases its own spiritual death on an instalment plan.

II

But we must not stop with the cultivation of a tough mind. The gospel also demands a tender heart. Toughmindedness without tenderheartedness is cold and detached, leaving one's life in a perpetual winter devoid of the warmth of spring and the gentle heat of summer. What is more tragic than to see a person who has risen to the disciplined heights of toughmindedness but has at the same time sunk to the passionless depths of hardheartedness?

The hardhearted person never truly loves. He engages in a crass utilitarianism which values other people mainly according to their usefulness to him. He never experiences the beauty of friendship, because he is too cold to feel affection for another and is too self-centred to share another's joy and sorrow. He is an isolated island. No outpouring of love links him with the mainland of humanity.

The hardhearted person lacks the capacity for genuine compassion. He is unmoved by the pains and afflictions of his brothers. He passes unfortunate men every day, but he never really sees them. He gives dollars to a worthwhile charity, but he gives not of his spirit.

The hardhearted individual never sees people as people, but rather as mere objects or as impersonal cogs in an ever-turning wheel. In the vast wheel of industry, he sees men as hands. In the massive wheel of big city life, he sees men as digits in a multitude. In the deadly wheel of army life, he sees men as numbers in a regiment. He depersonalizes life.

Jesus frequently illustrated the characteristics of the hardhearted. The rich fool was condemned, not because he was not toughminded, but rather because he was not tenderhearted. Life for him was a mirror in which he saw only himself, and not a window through which he saw other selves. Dives went to hell, not because he was wealthy, but because he was not tenderhearted enough to see Lazarus and because he made no attempt to bridge the gulf between himself and his brother.

Jesus reminds us that the good life combines the toughness of the serpent and the tenderness of the dove. To have serpentlike qualities devoid of dovelike qualities is to be passionless, mean, and selfish. To have dovelike without serpentlike qualities is to be sentimental, anæmic, and aimless. We must combine strongly marked antitheses.

We as Negroes must bring together toughmindedness and tenderheartedness, if we are to move creatively toward the goal of freedom and justice. Softminded individuals among us feel that the only way to deal with oppression is by adjusting to it. They acquiesce and resign themselves to segregation. They prefer to remain oppressed. When Moses led the children of Israel from the slavery of Egypt to the freedom of the Promised Land, he discovered that slaves do not always welcome their deliverers. They would rather bear those ills they have, as Shakespeare pointed out, than flee to others that they know not of. They prefer the "fleshpots of Egypt" to the ordeals of emancipation. But this is not the way out. Softminded acquiescence is cowardly. My friends, we cannot win the respect of the white people of the South or elsewhere if we are willing to trade the future of our children for our personal safety and comfort. Moreover, we must learn that passively to accept an unjust system is to co-operate with that system, and thereby to become a participant in its evil.

And there are hardhearted and bitter individuals among us who would combat the opponent with physical violence and corroding hatred. Violence brings only temporary victories; violence, by creating many more social problems than it solves, never brings permanent peace. I am convinced that if we succumb to the temptation to use violence in our struggle for freedom, unborn generations will be the recipients of a long and desolate night of bitterness, and our chief legacy to them will be a never-ending reign of chaos. A Voice, echoing through the corridors of time, says to every intemperate Peter, "Put up thy sword." History is cluttered with the wreckage of nations that failed to follow Christ's command.

III

A third way is open to our quest for freedom, namely, nonviolent resistance, that combines toughmindedness and tenderheartedness and avoids the complacency and do-nothingness of the softminded and the violence and bitterness of the hardhearted. My belief is that this method must guide our action in the present crisis in race relations. Through nonviolent resistance we shall be able to oppose the unjust system and at the same time love the perpetrators of the system. We must work passionately and unrelentingly for full stature as citizens, but may it never be said, my friends, that to gain it we used the inferior methods of falsehood, malice, hate, and violence.

I would not conclude without applying the meaning of the text to the nature of God. The greatness of our God lies in the fact that he is both toughminded and tenderhearted. He has qualities both of austerity and of gentleness. The Bible, always clear in stressing both attributes of God, expresses his toughmindedness in his justice and wrath and his tenderheartedness in his love and grace. God has two outstretched arms. One is strong enough to surround us with justice, and one is gentle enough to embrace us with grace. On the one hand, God is a God of justice who punished Israel for her wayward deeds, and on the other hand, he is a forgiving father whose heart was filled with unutterable joy when the prodigal returned home.

I am thankful that we worship a God who is both toughminded and tenderhearted. If God were only toughminded, he would be a cold, passionless despot sitting in some far-off heaven "contemplating all," as Tennyson puts it in "The Palace of Art." He would be Aristotle's "unmoved mover," self-knowing, but not other-loving. But if God were only tenderhearted, he would be too soft and sentimental to function when things go wrong and incapable of controlling what he has made. He would be like H. G. Wells's lovable God in *God, the Invisible King*, who is strongly desirous of making a good world, but finds himself helpless before the surging powers of evil. God is neither hardhearted nor softminded. He is toughminded enough to transcend the world; he is tenderhearted enough to live in it. He does not leave us alone in our agonies and struggles. He seeks us in dark places and suffers with us and for us in our tragic prodigality.

At times we need to know that the Lord is a God of justice. When slumbering giants of injustice emerge in the earth, we need to know that there is a God of power who can cut them down like the grass and leave them withering like the green herb. When our most tireless efforts fail to stop the surging sweep of oppression, we need to know that in this universe is a God whose matchless strength is a fit contrast to the sordid weakness of man. But there are also times when we need to know that God possesses love and mercy. When we are staggered by the chilly winds of adversity and battered by the raging storms of disappointment and when through our folly and sin we stray into some destructive far country and are frustrated because of a strange feeling of homesickness, we need to know that there is Someone who loves us, cares for us, understands us, and will give us another chance. When days grow dark and nights grow dreary, we can be thankful that our God combines in his nature a creative synthesis of love and justice which will lead us through life's dark valleys and into sunlit pathways of hope and fulfilment.

CHAPTER TWO

Transformed nonconformist

*Be not conformed to this world: but be
ye transformed by the renewing of your
mind.*   Romans 12:2

"Do not conform" is difficult advice in a generation when
crowd pressures have unconsciously conditioned our minds
and feet to move to the rhythmic drumbeat of the status quo.
Many voices and forces urge us to choose the path of least
resistance, and bid us never to fight for an unpopular cause
and never to be found in a pathetic minority of two or
three.

Even certain of our intellectual disciplines persuade us
of the need to conform. Some philosophical sociologists
suggest that morality is merely group consensus and that the
folkways are the right ways. Some psychologists say that
mental and emotional adjustment is the reward of thinking
and acting like other people.

Success, recognition, and conformity are the bywords of
the modern world where everyone seems to crave the anæs-
thetizing security of being identified with the majority.

I

In spite of this prevailing tendency to conform, we as
Christians have a mandate to be nonconformists. The Apostle
Paul, who knew the inner realities of the Christian faith,

counselled, "Be not conformed to this world: but be ye transformed by the renewing of your mind." We are called to be people of conviction, not conformity; of moral nobility, not social respectability. We are commanded to live differently and according to a higher loyalty.

Every true Christian is a citizen of two worlds, the world of time and the world of eternity. We are, paradoxically, in the world and yet not of the world. To the Philippian Christians, Paul wrote, "We are a colony of heaven." They understood what he meant, for their city of Philippi was a Roman colony. When Rome wished to Romanize a province, she established a small colony of people who lived by Roman law and Roman customs and who, though in another country, held fast to their Roman allegiance. This powerful, creative minority spread the gospel of Roman culture. Although the analogy is imperfect—the Roman settlers lived within a framework of injustice and exploitation, that is, colonialism —the Apostle does point to the responsibility of Christians to imbue an unchristian world with the ideals of a higher and more noble order. Living in the colony of time, we are ultimately responsible to the empire of eternity. As Christians we must never surrender our supreme loyalty to any time-bound custom or earth-bound idea, for at the heart of our universe is a higher reality—God and his kingdom of love— to which we must be conformed.

This command not to conform comes, not only from Paul, but also from our Lord and Master, Jesus Christ, the world's most dedicated nonconformist, whose ethical nonconformity still challenges the conscience of mankind.

When an affluent society would coax us to believe that happiness consists in the size of our automobiles, the impressiveness of our houses, and the expensiveness of our clothes, Jesus reminds us, "A man's life consisteth not in the abundance of the things which he possesseth."

When we would yield to the temptation of a world rife with sexual promiscuity and gone wild with a philosophy of self-expression, Jesus tells us that "whosoever looketh on a woman to lust after her hath committed adultery with her already in his heart."

When we refuse to suffer for righteousness and choose to follow the path of comfort rather than conviction, we hear Jesus say, "Blessed are they which are persecuted for righteousness' sake: for theirs is the kingdom of heaven."

When in our spiritual pride we boast of having reached the peak of moral excellence, Jesus warns, "The publicans and the harlots go into the kingdom of God before you."

When we, through compassionless detachment and arrogant individualism, fail to respond to the needs of the underprivileged, the Master says, "Inasmuch as ye have done it unto one of the least of these my brethren, ye have done it unto me."

When we allow the spark of revenge in our souls to flame up in hate toward our enemies, Jesus teaches, "Love your enemies, bless them that curse you, do good to them that hate you, and pray for them which despitefully use you, and persecute you."

Everywhere and at all times, the love ethic of Jesus is a radiant light revealing the ugliness of our stale conformity.

In spite of this imperative demand to live differently, we have cultivated a mass mind and have moved from the extreme of rugged individualism to the even greater extreme of rugged collectivism. We are not makers of history; we are made by history. Longfellow said, "In this world a man must either be anvil or hammer," meaning that he is either a moulder of society or is moulded by society. Who doubts that today most men are anvils and are shaped by the patterns of the majority? Or to change the figure, most people, and Christians in particular, are thermometers that record or register the temperature of majority opinion, not thermostats that transform and regulate the temperature of society.

Many people fear nothing more terribly than to take a position which stands out sharply and clearly from the prevailing opinion. The tendency of most is to adopt a view that is so ambiguous that it will include everything and so popular that it will include everybody. Along with this has grown an inordinate worship of bigness. We live in an age of "jumboism" where men find security in that which is large and extensive—big cities, big buildings, big corporations. This worship of size has caused many to fear being identified with a minority idea. Not a few men, who cherish lofty and noble ideals, hide them under a bushel for fear of being called different. Many sincere white people in the South privately oppose segregation and discrimination, but they are apprehensive lest they be publicly condemned. Millions of citizens are deeply disturbed that the military-industrial complex too often shapes national policy, but they do not want to be considered unpatriotic. Countless loyal Americans honestly feel that a world body such as the United Nations should include even Red China, but they fear being called Communist sympathizers. A legion of thoughtful persons recognizes that traditional capitalism must continually undergo change if our great national wealth is to be more equitably distributed, but they are afraid their criticisms will make them seem un-American. Numerous decent, wholesome young persons permit themselves to become involved in unwholesome pursuits which they do not personally condone or even enjoy, because they are ashamed to say no when the gang says yes. How *few* people have the audacity to express publicly their convictions, and how *many* have allowed themselves to be "astronomically intimidated"!

Blind conformity makes us so suspicious of an individual who insists on saying what he really believes that we recklessly threaten his civil liberties. If a man, who believes vigorously in peace, is foolish enough to carry a sign in a public demonstration, or if a Southern white person, believing in the American dream of the dignity and worth of human personality, dares to invite a Negro into his home and join with him in his struggle for freedom, he is liable to be summoned before some legislative investigation body. He most certainly is a Communist if he espouses the cause of human brotherhood!

Thomas Jefferson wrote, "I have sworn upon the altar of God eternal hostility against every form of tyranny over the mind of man." To the conformist and the shapers of the conformist mentality, this must surely sound like a

most dangerous and radical doctrine. Have we permitted the
lamp of independent thought and individualism to become
so dim that were Jefferson to write and live by these words
today we would find cause to harass and investigate him?
If Americans permit thought-control, business-control, and
freedom-control to continue, we shall surely move within the
shadows of fascism.

II

Nowhere is the tragic tendency to conform more evident
than in the church, an institution which has often served
to crystallize, conserve, and even bless the patterns of
majority opinion. The erstwhile sanction by the church of
slavery, racial segregation, war, and economic exploitation
is testimony to the fact that the church has hearkened more
to the authority of the world than to the authority of God.
Called to be the moral guardian of the community, the
church at times has preserved that which is immoral and
unethical. Called to combat social evils, it has remained
silent behind stained-glass windows. Called to lead men
on the highway of brotherhood and to summon them to
rise above the narrow confines of race and class, it has
enunciated and practised racial exclusiveness.

We preachers have also been tempted by the enticing
cult of conformity. Seduced by the success symbols of the
world, we have measured our achievements by the size of our
parsonage. We have become showmen to please the whims
and caprices of the people. We preach comforting sermons
and avoid saying anything from our pulpit which might dis-
turb the respectable views of the comfortable members of
our congregations. Have we ministers of Jesus Christ sacrificed truth on the altar of self-interest and, like Pilate,
yielded our convictions to the demands of the crowd?

We need to recapture the gospel glow of the early Christians, who were nonconformists in the truest sense of the
word and refused to shape their witness according to the
mundane patterns of the world. Willingly they sacrificed

fame, fortune, and life itself in behalf of a cause they knew
to be right. Quantitatively small, they were qualitatively
giants. Their powerful gospel put an end to such barbaric
evils as infanticide and bloody gladiatorial contests. Finally,
they captured the Roman Empire for Jesus Christ.

Gradually, however, the church became so entrenched in
wealth and prestige that it began to dilute the strong demands
of the gospel and to conform to the ways of the world.
And ever since the church has been a weak and ineffectual
trumpet making uncertain sounds. If the church of Jesus
Christ is to regain once more its power, message, and
authentic ring, it must conform only to the demands of the
gospel.

The hope of a secure and livable world lies with disciplined
nonconformists, who are dedicated to justice, peace, and
brotherhood. The trailblazers in human, academic, scientific,
and religious freedom have always been nonconformists. In
any cause that concerns the progress of mankind, put your
faith in the nonconformist!

In his essay "Self-Reliance" Emerson wrote, "Whoso
would be a man must be a nonconformist." The Apostle
Paul reminds us that whoso would be a Christian must also
be a nonconformist. Any Christian who blindly accepts
the opinions of the majority and in fear and timidity follows
a path of expediency and social approval is a mental and
spiritual slave. Mark well these words from the pen of
James Russell Lowell:

> They are slaves who fear to speak
> For the fallen and the weak;
> They are slaves who will not choose
> Hatred, scoffing, and abuse,
> Rather than in silence shrink
> From the truth they needs must think;
> They are slaves who dare not be
> In the right with two or three.

III

Nonconformity in itself, however, may not necessarily be good and may at times possess neither transforming nor redemptive power. Nonconformity per se contains no saving value, and may represent in some circumstances little more than a form of exhibitionism. Paul in the latter half of the text offers a formula for constructive nonconformity: "Be ye transformed by the renewing of your mind." Nonconformity is creative when it is controlled and directed by a transformed life and is constructive when it embraces a new mental outlook. By opening our lives to God in Christ we become new creatures. This experience, which Jesus spoke of as the new birth, is essential if we are to be transformed nonconformists and freed from the cold hardheartedness and self-righteousness so often characteristic of nonconformity. Someone has said, "I love reforms but I hate reformers." A reformer may be an untransformed nonconformist whose rebellion against the evils of society has left him annoyingly rigid and unreasonably impatient.

Only through an inner spiritual transformation do we gain the strength to fight vigorously the evils of the world in a humble and loving spirit. The transformed nonconformist, moreover, never yields to the passive sort of patience which is an excuse to do nothing. And this very transformation saves him from speaking irresponsible words which estrange without reconciling and from making hasty judgments which are blind to the necessity of social progress. He recognizes that social change will not come overnight, yet he works as though it is an imminent possibility.

This hour in history needs a dedicated circle of transformed nonconformists. Our planet teeters on the brink of atomic annihilation; dangerous passions of pride, hatred, and selfishness are enthroned in our lives; truth lies prostrate on the rugged hills of nameless calvaries; and men do reverence before false gods of nationalism and materialism. The saving of our world from pending doom will come, not through the complacent adjustment of the conforming majority, but through the creative maladjustment of a non-conforming minority.

Some years ago Professor Bixler reminded us of the danger of overstressing the well-adjusted life. Everybody passionately seeks to be well-adjusted. We must, of course, be well-adjusted if we are to avoid neurotic and schizophrenic personalities, but there are some things in our world to which men of goodwill must be maladjusted. I confess that I never intend to become adjusted to the evils of segregation and the crippling effects of discrimination, to the moral degeneracy of religious bigotry and the corroding effects of narrow sectarianism, to economic conditions that deprive men of work and food, and to the insanities of militarism and the self-defeating effects of physical violence.

Human salvation lies in the hands of the creatively maladjusted. We need today maladjusted men like Shadrach, Meshach, and Abednego, who, when ordered by King Nebuchadnezzar to bow before a golden image, said in unequivocal terms, "If it be so, our God whom we serve is able to deliver us. . . . But if not . . . we will not serve thy gods"; like Thomas Jefferson, who in an age adjusted to slavery wrote, "We hold these truths to be self-evident, that all men are created equal, that they are endowed by their Creator with certain unalienable Rights, that among these are Life, Liberty and the pursuit of Happiness"; like Abraham Lincoln, who had the wisdom to discern that this nation could not survive half slave and half free; and supremely like our Lord, who, in the midst of the intricate and fascinating military machinery of the Roman Empire, reminded his disciples that "they that take the sword shall perish with the sword." Through such maladjustment an already decadent generation may be called to those things which make for peace.

Honesty impels me to admit that transformed nonconformity, which is always costly and never altogether comfortable, may mean walking through the valley of the shadow of suffering, losing a job, or having a six-year-old daughter ask, "Daddy, why do you have to go to jail so much?" But we are gravely mistaken to think that Christianity protects us from the pain and agony of mortal existence. Christianity has always insisted that the cross we bear precedes the crown we wear. To be a Christian, one must take up his cross, with all of its difficulties and agonizing and tragedy-packed content, and carry it until that very cross leaves its marks upon us and redeems us to that more excellent way which comes only through suffering.

In these days of worldwide confusion, there is a dire need for men and women who will courageously do battle for truth. We need Christians who will echo the words John Bunyan said to his jailer when, having spent twelve years in jail, he was promised freedom if he would agree to stop preaching:

But if nothing will do, unless I make of my conscience a continual butchery and slaughter-shop. unless, putting out my own eyes, I commit me to the blind to lead me, as I doubt is desired by some, I have determined, the Almighty God being my help and shield, yet to suffer, if frail life might continue so long, even till the moss shall grow on mine eyebrows, rather than thus to violate my faith and principles.

We must make a choice. Will we continue to march to the drumbeat of conformity and respectability, or will we, listening to the beat of a more distant drum, move to its echoing sounds? Will we march only to the music of time, or will we, risking criticism and abuse, march to the soul-saving music of eternity? More than ever before we are today challenged by the words of yesterday, "Be not conformed to this world: but be ye transformed by the renewing of your mind."

CHAPTER THREE

On being a good neighbour

And who is my neighbour? Luke 10:29

I should like to talk with you about a good man, whose exemplary life will always be a flashing light to plague the dozing conscience of mankind. His goodness was not found in a passive commitment to a particular creed, but in his active participation in a life-saving deed; not in a moral pilgrimage that reached its destination point, but in the love ethic by which he journeyed life's highway. He was good because he was a good neighbour.

The ethical concern of this man is expressed in a magnificent little story, which begins with a theological discussion on the meaning of eternal life and concludes in a concrete expression of compassion on a dangerous road. Jesus is asked a question by a man who had been trained in the details of Jewish law: "Master, what shall I do to inherit eternal life?" The retort is prompt: "What is written in the law? how readest thou?" After a moment the lawyer recites articulately: "Thou shalt love the Lord thy God with all thy heart, and with all thy soul, and with all thy strength, and with all thy mind; and thy neighbour as thyself." Then comes the decisive word from Jesus: "Thou hast answered right: this do, and thou shalt live."

The lawyer was chagrined. "Why," the people might ask, "would an expert in law raise a question that even the novice can answer?" Desiring to justify himself and to show that Jesus' reply was far from conclusive, the lawyer asks,

"And who is my neighbour?" The lawyer was now taking up the cudgels of debate that might have turned the conversation into an abstract theological discussion. But Jesus, determined not to be caught in the "paralysis of analysis," pulls the question from mid-air and places it on a dangerous curve between Jerusalem and Jericho.

He told the story of "a certain man" who went down from Jerusalem to Jericho and fell among robbers who stripped him, beat him, and, departing, left him half dead. By chance a certain priest appeared, but he passed by on the other side, and later a Levite also passed by. Finally, a certain Samaritan, a half-breed from a people with whom the Jews had no dealings, appeared. When he saw the wounded man, he was moved with compassion, administered first aid, placed him on his beast, "and brought him to an inn, and took care of him."

Who is my neighbour? "I do not know his name," says Jesus in essence. "He is anyone toward whom you are neighbourly. He is anyone who lies in need at life's roadside. He is neither Jew nor Gentile; he is neither Russian nor American; he is neither Negro nor white. He is 'a certain man'—any needy man—on one of the numerous Jericho roads of life." So Jesus defines a neighbour, not in a theological definition, but in a life situation.

What constituted the goodness of the good Samaritan? Why will he always be an inspiring paragon of neighbourly virtue? It seems to me that this man's goodness may be described in one word—altruism. The good Samaritan was altruistic to the core. What is altruism? The dictionary defines altruism as "regard for, and devotion to, the interest of others." The Samaritan was good because he made concern for others the first law of his life.

I

The Samaritan had the capacity for a *universal altruism*. He had a piercing insight into that which is beyond the eternal accidents of race, religion, and nationality. One of the great tragedies of man's long trek along the highway of history has been the limiting of neighbourly concern to tribe, race, class, or nation. The God of early Old Testament days was a tribal god and the ethic was tribal. "Thou shalt not kill" meant "Thou shalt not kill a fellow Israelite, but for God's sake, kill a Philistine." Greek democracy embraced a certain aristocracy, but not the hordes of Greek slaves whose labours built the city-states. The universalism at the centre of the Declaration of Independence has been shamefully negated by America's appalling tendency to substitute "some" for "all." Numerous people in the North and South still believe that the affirmation, "All men are created equal," means "All white men are created equal." Our unswerving devotion to monopolistic capitalism makes us more concerned about the economic security of the captains of industry than for the labouring men whose sweat and skills keep industry functioning.

What are the devastating consequences of this narrow, group-centred attitude? It means that one does not really mind what happens to the people outside his group. If an American is concerned only about his nation, he will not be concerned about the peoples of Asia, Africa, or South America. Is this not why nations engage in the madness of war without the slightest sense of penitence? Is this not why the murder of a citizen of your own nation is a crime, but the murder of the citizens of another nation in war is an act of heroic virtue? If manufacturers are concerned only in their personal interests, they will pass by on the other side while thousands of working people are stripped of their jobs and left displaced on some Jericho road as a result of automation, and they will judge every move toward a better distribution of wealth and a better life for the working man to be socialistic. If a white man is concerned only about his race, he will casually pass by the Negro who has been robbed of his personhood, stripped of his sense of dignity, and left dying on some wayside road.

A few years ago, when an automobile carrying several members of a Negro college basketball team had an accident on a Southern highway, three of the young men were severely injured. An ambulance was immediately called, but on arriving at the place of the accident, the driver, who was white, said without apology that it was not his policy to service Negroes, and he drove away. The driver of a passing automobile graciously drove the boys to the nearest hospital, but the attending physician belligerently said, "We don't take niggers in this hospital." When the boys finally arrived at a "coloured" hospital in a town some fifty miles from the scene of the accident, one was dead and the other two died thirty and fifty minutes later respectively. Probably all three could have been saved if they had been given immediate treatment. This is only one of thousands of in-human incidents that occur daily in the South, an unbeliev-able expression of the barbaric consequences of any tribal-centred, national-centred, or racial-centred ethic.

The real tragedy of such narrow provincialism is that we see people as entities or merely as things. Too seldom do we see people in their true *humanness*. A spiritual myopia limits our vision to external accidents. We see men as Jews or Gentiles, Catholics or Protestants, Chinese or American, Negroes or whites. We fail to think of them as fellow human beings made from the same basic stuff as we, moulded in the same divine image. The priest and the Levite saw only a bleeding body, not a human being like themselves. But the good Samaritan will always remind us to remove the cata-racts of provincialism from our spiritual eyes and see men as men. If the Samaritan had considered the wounded man as a Jew first, he would not have stopped, for the Jews and the Samaritans had no dealings. He saw him as a human being first, who was a Jew only by accident. The good neighbour looks beyond the external accidents and discerns those inner qualities that make all men human and, there-fore, brothers.

II

The Samaritan possessed the capacity for a *dangerous altruism*. He risked his life to save a brother. When we ask why the priest and the Levite did not stop to help the wounded man, numerous suggestions come to mind. Perhaps they could not delay their arrival at an important ecclesiastical meeting. Perhaps religious regulations demanded that they touch no human body for several hours prior to the performing of their temple functions. Or perhaps they were on their way to an organizational meeting of a Jericho Road Improvement Association. Certainly this would have been a real need, for it is not enough to aid a wounded man on the Jericho Road; it is also important to change the conditions which make robbery possible. Philanthropy is commendable, but it must not cause the philanthropist to overlook the circumstances of economic injustice which make philanthropy necessary. Maybe the priest and the Levite believed that it is better to cure injustice at the causal source than to get bogged down with a single individual effect.

These are probable reasons for their failure to stop, yet there is another possibility, often overlooked, that they were afraid. The Jericho Road was a dangerous road. When Mrs. King and I visited the Holy Land, we rented a car and drove from Jerusalem to Jericho. As we travelled slowly down that meandering, mountainous road, I said to my wife, "I can now understand why Jesus chose this road as the setting for his parable." Jerusalem is some two thousand feet above and Jericho one thousand feet below sea level. The descent is made in less than twenty miles. Many sudden curves provide likely places for ambushing and expose the traveller to unforeseen attacks. Long ago the road was known as the Bloody Pass. So it is possible that the priest and the Levite were afraid that if they stopped, they too would be beaten. Perhaps the robbers were still nearby. Or maybe the wounded man on the ground was a faker, who wished to draw passing travellers to his side for quick and easy seizure. I imagine that the first question which the priest and the Levite asked was: "If I stop to help this man, what will happen to me?" But by the very nature of his concern, the good Samaritan reversed the question: "If I do not stop to help this man, what will happen to him?" The good Samaritan engaged in a dangerous altruism.

We so often ask, "What will happen to my job, my prestige, or my status if I take a stand on this issue? Will my home be bombed, will my life be threatened, or will I be jailed?" The good man always reverses the question. Albert Schweitzer did not ask, "What will happen to my prestige and security as a university professor and to my status as a Bach organist, if I work with the people of Africa?" but rather he asked, "What will happen to these millions of people who have been wounded by the forces of injustice, if I do not go to them?" Abraham Lincoln did not ask, "What will happen to me if I issue the Emancipation Proclamation and bring an end to chattel slavery?" but he asked, "What will happen to the Union and to millions of Negro people, if I fail to do it?" The Negro professional does not ask, "What will happen to my secure position, my middle-class status, or my personal safety, if I participate in the movement to end the system of segregation?" but "What will happen to the cause of justice and the masses of Negro people who have never experienced the warmth of economic security, if I do not participate actively and courageously in the movement?"

The ultimate measure of a man is not where he stands in moments of comfort and convenience, but where he stands at times of challenge and controversy. The true neighbour will risk his position, his prestige, and even his life for the welfare of others. In dangerous valleys and hazardous pathways, he will lift some bruised and beaten brother to a higher and more noble life.

III

The Samaritan also possessed *excessive altruism*. With his own hands he bound the wounds of the man and then set him on his own beast. It would have been easier to pay an ambulance to take the unfortunate man to the hospital, rather than risk having his neatly trimmed suit stained with blood.

True altruism is more than the capacity to pity; it is the

capacity to sympathize. Pity may represent little more than the impersonal concern which prompts the mailing of a cheque, but true sympathy is the personal concern which demands the giving of one's soul. Pity may arise from interest in an abstraction called humanity, but sympathy grows out of a concern for a particular needy human being who lies at life's roadside. Sympathy is fellow feeling for the person in need—his pain, agony, and burdens. Our missionary efforts fail when they are based on pity, rather than true compassion. Instead of seeking to do something *with* the African and Asian peoples, we have too often sought only to do something *for* them. An expression of pity devoid of genuine sympathy, leads to a new form of paternalism which no self-respecting person can accept. Dollars possess the potential for helping wounded children of God on life's Jericho Road, but unless those dollars are distributed by compassionate fingers they will enrich neither the giver nor the receiver. Millions of missionary dollars have gone to Africa from the hands of church people who would die a million deaths before they would permit a single African the privilege of worshipping in their congregation. Millions of Peace Corps dollars are being invested in Africa because of the votes of some men who fight unrelentingly to prevent African ambassadors from holding membership in their diplomatic clubs or establishing residency in their particular neighbourhoods. The Peace Corps will fail if it seeks to do something *for* the underprivileged peoples of the world; it will succeed if it seeks creatively to do something *with* them. It will fail as a negative gesture to defeat Communism; it will succeed only as a positive effort to wipe poverty, ignorance, and disease from the earth. Money devoid of love is like salt devoid of savour, good for nothing except to be trodden under the foot of men. True neighbourliness requires personal concern. The Samaritan used his hands to bind up the wounds of the robbed man's body, and he also released an overflowing love to bind up the wounds of his broken spirit.

Another expression of the excessive altruism on the part of the Samaritan was his willingness to go far beyond the call of duty. After tending to the man's wounds, he put him on his beast, carried him to an inn, and left money for his care, making clear that if further financial needs arose he would gladly meet them. "Whatsoever thou spendest more, when I come again, I will repay thee." Stopping short of this, he would have more than fulfilled any possible rule concerning one's duty to a wounded stranger. He went beyond the second mile. His love was complete.

Dr. Harry Emerson Fosdick has made an impressive distinction between enforceable and unenforceable obligations. The former are regulated by the codes of society and the vigorous implementation of law-enforcement agencies. Breaking these obligations, spelled out on thousands of pages in law books, has filled numerous prisons. But unenforceable obligations are beyond the reach of the laws of society. They concern inner attitudes, genuine person-to-person relations, and expressions of compassion which law books cannot regulate and jails cannot rectify. Such obligations are met by one's commitment to an inner law, written on the heart. Man-made laws assure justice, but a higher law produces love. No code of conduct ever persuaded a father to love his children or a husband to show affection to his wife. The law court may force him to provide bread for the family, but it cannot make him provide the bread of love. A good father is obedient to the unenforceable. The good Samaritan represents the conscience of mankind because he also was obedient to that which could not be enforced. No law in the world could have produced such unalloyed compassion, such genuine love, such thorough altruism.

In our nation today a mighty struggle is taking place. It is a struggle to conquer the reign of an evil monster called segregation and its inseparable twin called discrimination— a monster that has wandered through this land for well-nigh one hundred years, stripping millions of Negro people of their sense of dignity and robbing them of their birthright of freedom.

Let us never succumb to the temptation of believing that legislation and judicial decrees play only minor roles in solving this problem. Morality cannot be legislated, but behaviour can be regulated. Judicial decrees may not change the heart, but they can restrain the heartless. The law cannot make an employer love an employee, but it can prevent him from refusing to hire me because of the colour of my skin. The habits, if not the hearts, of people have been and are being altered every day by legislative acts, judicial decisions, and executive orders. Let us not be misled by those who argue that segregation cannot be ended by the force of law.

But acknowledging this, we must admit that the ultimate solution to the race problem lies in the willingness of men to obey the unenforceable. Court orders and federal enforcement agencies are of inestimable value in achieving desegregation, but desegregation is only a partial, though necessary, step toward the final goal which we seek to realize, genuine intergroup and interpersonal living. Desegregation will break down the legal barriers and bring men together physically, but something must touch the hearts and souls of men so that they will come together spiritually because it is natural and right. A vigorous enforcement of civil rights laws will bring an end to segregated public facilities which are barriers to a truly desegregated society, but it cannot bring an end to fears, prejudice, pride, and irrationality, which are the barriers to a truly integrated society. These dark and demonic responses will be removed only as men are possessed by the invisible, inner law which etches on their hearts the conviction that all men are brothers and that love is mankind's most potent weapon for personal and social transformation. True integration will be achieved by true neighbours who are willingly obedient to unenforceable obligations.

More than ever before, my friends, men of all races and nations are today challenged to be neighbourly. The call for a worldwide good-neighbour policy is more than an ephemeral shibboleth; it is the call to a way of life which will transform our imminent cosmic elegy into a psalm of creative fulfilment. No longer can we afford the luxury of passing by on the other side. Such folly was once called moral failure; today it will lead to universal suicide. We cannot long survive spiritually separated in a world that is geographically together. In - the final analysis, I must not ignore the wounded man on life's Jericho Road, because he is a part of me and I am a part of him. His agony diminishes me, and his salvation enlarges me.

In our quest to make neighbourly love a reality, we have, in addition to the inspiring example of the good Samaritan, the magnanimous life of our Christ to guide us. His altruism was universal, for he thought of all men, even publicans and sinners, as brothers. His altruism was dangerous, for he willingly travelled hazardous roads in a cause he knew was right. His altruism was excessive, for he chose to die on Calvary, history's most magnificent expression of obedience to the unenforceable.

CHAPTER FOUR

Love in action

Then said Jesus, Father, forgive them;
for they know not what they do.
                    Luke 23:34

Few words in the New Testament more clearly and solemnly express the magnanimity of Jesus' spirit than that sublime utterance from the cross, "Father, forgive them; for they know not what they do." This is love at its best.

We shall not fully understand the great meaning of Jesus' prayer unless we first notice that the text opens with the word "then." The verse immediately preceding reads thus: "And when they were come to the place, which is called Calvary, there they crucified him, and the malefactors, one on the right hand, and the other on the left." Then said Jesus, "Father, forgive them." *Then*—when he was being plunged into the abyss of nagging agony. *Then*—when man had stooped to his worst. *Then*—when he was dying, a most ignominious death. *Then*—when the wicked hands of the creature had dared to crucify the only begotten Son of the Creator. Then said Jesus, "Father, forgive them." That "then" might well have been otherwise. He could have said, "Father, get even with them," or "Father, let loose the mighty thunderbolts of righteous wrath and destroy them," or "Father, open the flood gates of justice and permit the staggering avalanche of retribution to pour upon them." But none of these was his response. Though subjected to inexpressible agony, suffering excruciating pain, and despised and rejected, nevertheless, he cried, "Father, forgive them."

Let us take note of two basic lessons to be gleaned from this text.

I

First, it is a marvellous expression of Jesus' ability to match words with actions. One of the great tragedies of life is that men seldom bridge the gulf between practice and profession, between doing and saying. A persistent schizophrenia leaves so many of us tragically divided against ourselves. On the one hand, we proudly profess certain sublime and noble principles, but on the other hand, we sadly practise the very antithesis of those principles. How often are our lives characterized by a high blood pressure of creeds and an anæmia of deeds! We talk eloquently about our commitment to the principles of Christianity, and yet our lives are saturated with the practices of paganism. We proclaim our devotion to democracy, but we sadly practise the very opposite of the democratic creed. We talk passionately about peace, and at the same time we assiduously prepare for war. We make our fervent pleas for the high road of justice, and then we tread unflinchingly the low road of injustice. This strange dichotomy, this agonizing gulf between the *ought* and the *is*, represents the tragic theme of man's earthly pilgrimage.

But in the life of Jesus we find that the gulf is bridged. Never in history was there a more sublime example of the consistency of word and deed. During his ministry in the sunny villages of Galilee, Jesus talked passionately about forgiveness. This strange doctrine awakened the questioning mind of Peter. "How oft," he asked, "shall my brother sin against me, and I forgive him? till seven times?" Peter wanted to be legal and statistical. But Jesus responded by affirming that there is no limit to forgiveness. "I say not unto thee, Until seven times: but, Until seventy times seven." In other words, forgiveness is not a matter of quantity, but of quality. A man cannot forgive up to four hundred and ninety times without forgiveness becoming a part of the habit structure of his being. Forgiveness is not an occasional act; it is a permanent attitude.

Jesus also admonished his followers to love their enemies and to pray for them that despitefully used them. This teaching fell upon the ears of many of his hearers like a strange music from a foreign land. Their ears were not attuned to the tonal qualities of such amazing love. They had been taught to love their friends and hate their enemies. Their lives had been conditioned to seek redress in the time-honoured tradition of retaliation. Yet Jesus taught them that only through a creative love for their enemies could they be children of their Father in heaven and also that love and forgiveness were absolute necessities for spiritual maturity.

The moment of testing emerges. Christ, the innocent Son of God, is stretched in painful agony on an uplifted cross. What place is there for love and forgiveness now? How will Jesus react? What will he say? The answer to these questions bursts forth in majestic splendour. Jesus lifts his thorn-crowned head and cries in words of cosmic proportions: "Father, forgive them; for they know not what they do." This was Jesus' finest hour; this was his heavenly response to his earthly rendezvous with destiny.

We sense the greatness of this prayer by contrasting it with nature, which, caught in the finality of her own impersonal structure, does not forgive. In spite of the agonizing pleas of men trapped in the path of an onrushing hurricane or the anguished cry of the builder falling from the scaffold, nature expresses only a cold, serene, and passionless indifference. She must honour everlastingly her fixed, immutable laws. When these laws are violated, she has no alternative except to follow inexorably her path of uniformity. Nature does not and cannot forgive.

Or contrast Jesus' prayer with the slowness of man to forgive. We live according to the philosophy that life is a matter of getting even and of saving face. We bow before the altar of revenge. Samson, eyeless at Gaza, prays fervently for his enemies—but only for their utter destruction.

The potential beauty of human life is constantly made ugly by man's ever-recurring song of retaliation.

Or contrast the prayer with a society that is even less prone to forgive. Society must have its standards, norms, and mores. It must have its legal checks and judicial restraints. Those who fall below the standard and those who disobey the laws are often left in a dark abyss of condemnation and have no hope for a second chance. Ask an innocent young lady, who, after a moment of overriding passion, becomes the mother of an illegitimate child. She will tell you that society is slow to forgive. Ask a public official, who, in a moment's carelessness, betrays the public trust. He will tell you that society is slow to forgive. Go to any prison and ask the inhabitants, who have written shameful lines across the pages of their lives. From behind the bars they will tell you that society is slow to forgive. Make your way to death row and speak with the tragic victims of criminality. As they prepare to make their pathetic walk to the electric chair, their hopeless cry is that society will not forgive. Capital punishment is society's final assertion that it will not forgive.

Such is the persistent story of mortal life. The oceans of history are made turbulent by the ever-rising tides of revenge. Man has never risen above the injunction of the *lex talionis*: "Life for life, eye for eye, tooth for tooth, hand for hand, foot for foot." In spite of the fact that the law of revenge solves no social problems, men continue to follow its disastrous leading. History is cluttered with the wreckage of nations and individuals that pursued this self-defeating path.

Jesus eloquently affirmed from the cross a higher law. He knew that the old eye-for-an-eye philosophy would leave everyone blind. He did not seek to overcome evil with evil. He overcame evil with good. Although crucified by hate, he responded with aggressive love.

What a magnificent lesson! Generations will rise and fall; men will continue to worship the god of revenge and bow before the altar of retaliation; but ever and again this noble lesson of Calvary will be a nagging reminder that only goodness can drive out evil and only love can conquer hate.

II

A second lesson comes to us from Jesus' prayer on the cross. It is an expression of Jesus' awareness of man's intellectual and spiritual blindness. "They know not what they do," said Jesus. Blindness was their trouble; enlightenment was their need. We must recognize that Jesus was nailed to the cross not simply by sin but also by blindness. The men who cried, "Crucify him," were not bad men but rather blind men. The jeering mob that lined the roadside which led to Calvary was composed not of evil people but of blind people. They knew not what they did. What a tragedy!

History reverberates with testimonies of this shameful tragedy. Centuries ago a sage named Socrates was forced to drink hemlock. The men who called for his death were not bad men with demonic blood running through their veins. On the contrary, they were sincere and respectable citizens of Greece. They genuinely thought that Socrates was an atheist because his idea of God had a philosophical depth that probed beyond traditional concepts. Not badness but blindness killed Socrates. Saul was not an evil-intentioned man when he persecuted Christians. He was a sincere, conscientious devotee of Israel's faith. He thought he was right. He persecuted Christians, not because he was devoid of integrity, but because he was devoid of enlightenment. The Christians who engaged in infamous persecutions and shameful inquisitions were not evil men but misguided men. The churchmen who felt that they had an edict from God to withstand the progress of science, whether in the form of a Copernican revolution or a Darwinian theory of natural selection, were not mischievous men but misinformed men. And so Christ's words from the cross are written in sharp-etched terms across some of the most inexpressible tragedies of history: "They know not what they do."

This tragic blindness expresses itself in many ominous ways in our own day. Some men still feel that war is the answer to the problems of the world. They are not evil people. On the contrary, they are good, respectable citizens whose ideas

are robed in the garments of patriotism. They talk of brink-
manship and a balance of terror. They sincerely feel that a
continuation of the arms race will be conducive to more
beneficent than maleficent consequences. So they passionately
call for bigger bombs, larger nuclear stockpiles, and faster
ballistic missiles.

Wisdom born of experience should tell us that war is
obsolete. There may have been a time when war served as a
negative good by preventing the spread and growth of an
evil force, but the destructive power of modern weapons
eliminates even the possibility that war may serve as a
negative good. If we assume that life is worth living and
that man has a right to survival, then we must find an alternative to war. In a day when vehicles hurtle through outer
space and guided ballistic missiles carve highways of death
through the stratosphere, no nation can claim victory in war.
A so-called limited war will leave little more than a calamitous legacy of human suffering, political turmoil, and spiritual disillusionment. A world war—God forbid!—will leave
only smouldering ashes as a mute testimony of a human
race whose folly led inexorably to untimely death. Yet there
are those who sincerely feel that disarmament is an evil
and international negotiation is an abominable waste of
time. Our world is threatened by the grim prospect of atomic
annihilation because there are still too many who know
not what they do.

Notice, too, how the truth of this text is revealed in race
relations. Slavery in America was perpetuated not merely by
human badness but also by human blindness. True, the
causal basis for the system of slavery must to a large extent
be traced back to the economic factor. Men convinced
themselves that a system which was so economically profitable must be morally justifiable. They formulated elaborate
theories of racial superiority. Their rationalizations clothed
obvious wrongs in the beautiful garments of righteousness.
This tragic attempt to give moral sanction to an economically profitable system gave birth to the doctrine of white
supremacy. Religion and the Bible were cited to crystallize
the status quo. Science was commandeered to prove the

biological inferiority of the Negro. Even philosophical logic was manipulated to give intellectual credence to the system of slavery. Someone formulated the argument of the inferiority of the Negro according to the framework of an Aristotelian syllogism:

> All men are made in the image of God;
> God, as everyone knows, is not a Negro;
> Therefore, the Negro is not a man.

So men conveniently twisted the insights of religion, science, and philosophy to give sanction to the doctrine of white supremacy. Soon this idea was imbedded in every textbook and preached in practically every pulpit. It became a structured part of the culture. And men then embraced this philosophy, not as the rationalization of a lie, but as the expression of a final truth. They sincerely came to believe that the Negro was inferior by nature and that slavery was ordained by God. In 1857, the system of slavery was given its greatest legal support by the deliberations of the Supreme Court of the United States in the Dred Scott decision. The Court affirmed that the Negro had no rights which the white man was bound to respect. The justices who rendered this decision were not wicked men. On the contrary, they were decent and dedicated men. But they were victims of spiritual and intellectual blindness. They knew not what they did. The whole system of slavery was largely perpetuated by sincere though spiritually ignorant persons.

This tragic blindness is also found in racial segregation, the not-too-distant cousin of slavery. Some of the most vigorous defenders of segregation are sincere in their beliefs and earnest in their motives. Although some men are segregationists merely for reasons of political expediency and economic gain, not all of the resistance to integration is the rear-guard of professional bigots. Some people feel that their attempt to preserve segregation is best for themselves, their children, and their nation. Many are good church people, anchored in the religious faith of their mothers and fathers. Pressed for a religious vindication for their conviction, they will even argue that God was the first segregationist. "Red birds and blue birds don't fly together," they contend. Their views about segregation, they insist, can be rationally explained and morally justified. Pressed for a justification of their belief in the inferiority of the Negro, they turn to some pseudo-scientific writing and argue that the Negro's brain is smaller than the white man's brain. They do not know, or they refuse to know, that the idea of an inferior or superior race has been refuted by the best evidence of the science of anthropology. Great anthropologists, like Ruth Benedict, Margaret Mead, and Melville J. Herskovits, agree that, although there may be inferior and superior individuals within all races, there is no superior or inferior race. And segregationists refuse to acknowledge that science has demonstrated that there are four types of blood and that these four types are found within every racial group. They blindly believe in the eternal validity of an evil called segregation and the timeless truth of a myth called white supremacy. What a tragedy! Millions of Negroes have been crucified by conscientious blindness. With Jesus on the cross, we must look lovingly at our oppressors and say, "Father, forgive them; for they know not what they do."

III

From all that I have attempted to say it should now be apparent that sincerity and conscientiousness in themselves are not enough. History has proven that these noble virtues may degenerate into tragic vices. Nothing in all the world is more dangerous than sincere ignorance and conscientious stupidity. Shakespeare wrote:

> For sweetest things turn sourest by their deeds;
> Lilies that fester smell far worse than weeds.

As the chief moral guardian of the community, the church must implore men to be good and well-intentioned and must extol the virtues of kindheartedness and conscientiousness. But somewhere along the way the church must remind men that devoid of intelligence, goodness and conscientiousness will become brutal forces leading to shameful crucifixions.

Never must the church tire of reminding men that they have a moral responsibility to be intelligent.

Must we not admit that the church has often overlooked this moral demand for enlightenment? At times it has talked as though ignorance were a virtue and intelligence a crime. Through its obscurantism, closedmindedness, and obstinacy to new truth, the church has often unconsciously encouraged its worshippers to look askance upon intelligence.

But if we are to call ourselves Christians, we had better avoid intellectual and moral blindness. Throughout the New Testament we are reminded of the need for enlightenment. We are commanded to love God, not only with our hearts and souls, but also with our minds. When the Apostle Paul noticed the blindness of many of his opponents, he said, "I bear them record that they have a zeal for God, but not according to knowledge." Over and again the Bible reminds us of the danger of zeal without knowledge and sincerity without intelligence.

So we have a mandate both to conquer sin and also to conquer ignorance. Modern man is presently having a rendezvous with chaos, not merely because of human badness, but also because of human stupidity. If Western civilization continues to degenerate until it, like twenty-four of its predecessors, falls hopelessly into a bottomless void, the cause will be not only its undeniable sinfulness, but also its appalling blindness. And if American democracy gradually disintegrates, it will be due as much to a lack of insight as to a lack of commitment to right. If modern man continues to flirt unhesitatingly with war and eventually transforms his earthly habitat into an inferno such as even the mind of Dante could not imagine, it will have resulted from downright badness and also from downright stupidity.

"They know not what they do," said Jesus. Blindness was their besetting trouble. And the crux of the matter lies here: we do need to be blind. Unlike physical blindness that is usually inflicted upon individuals as a result of natural forces beyond their control, intellectual and moral blindness is a dilemma which man inflicts upon himself by his tragic misuse of freedom and his failure to use his mind to its fullest capacity. One day we will learn that the heart can never be totally right if the head is totally wrong. Only through the bringing together of head and heart—intelligence and goodness—shall man rise to a fulfilment of his true nature. Neither is this to say that one must be a philosopher or a possessor of extensive academic training before he can achieve the good life. I know many people of limited formal training who have amazing intelligence and foresight. The call for intelligence is a call for openmindedness, sound judgment, and love for truth. It is a call for men to rise above the stagnation of closedmindedness and the paralysis of gullibility. One does not need to be a profound scholar to be openminded, nor a keen academician to engage in an assiduous pursuit for truth.

Light has come into the world. A voice crying through the vista of time calls men to walk in the light. Man's earthly life will become a tragic cosmic elegy if he fails to heed this call. "This is the condemnation," says John, "that light is come into the world, and men loved darkness rather than light."

Jesus was right about those men who crucified him. They knew not what they did. They were inflicted with a terrible blindness.

Every time I look at the cross I am reminded of the greatness of God and the redemptive power of Jesus Christ. I am reminded of the beauty of sacrificial love and the majesty of unswerving devotion to truth. It causes me to say with John Bowring:

> In the cross of Christ I glory,
> Towering o'er the wrecks of time;
> All the light of sacred story
> Gathers round its head sublime.

It would be wonderful were I to look at the cross and sense only such a sublime reaction. But somehow I can never turn my eyes from that cross without also realizing that it symbolizes a strange mixture of greatness and smallness, of good and evil. As I behold that uplifted cross I am reminded not only of the unlimited power of God, but also of the sordid weakness of man. I think not only of the radiance of the divine, but also of the tang of the human. I am reminded not only of Christ at his best, but of man at his worst.

We must see the cross as the magnificent symbol of love conquering hate and of light overcoming darkness. But in the midst of this glowing affirmation, let us never forget that our Lord and Master was nailed to that cross because of human blindness. Those who crucified him knew not what they did.

CHAPTER FIVE

Loving your enemies

*Ye have heard that it hath been said,
Thou shalt love thy neighbour, and hate
thine enemy. But I say unto you, Love
your enemies, bless them that curse you,
do good to them that hate you, and
pray for them which despitefully use
you, and persecute you; that ye may be
children of your Father which is in
heaven.* Matthew 5:43-45

Probably no admonition of Jesus has been more difficult to follow than the command to "love your enemies." Some men have sincerely felt that its actual practice is not possible. It is easy, they say, to love those who love you, but how can one love those who openly and insidiously seek to defeat you? Others, like the philosopher Nietzsche, contend that Jesus' exhortation to love one's enemies is testimony to the fact that the Christian ethic is designed for the weak and cowardly, and not for the strong and courageous. Jesus, they say, was an impractical idealist.

In spite of these insistent questions and persistent objections, this command of Jesus challenges us with new urgency. Upheaval after upheaval has reminded us that modern man is travelling along a road called hate, in a journey that will bring us to destruction and damnation. Far from being the pious injunction of a Utopian dreamer, the command to love one's enemy is an absolute necessity for our survival.

Love even for enemies is the key to the solution of the problems of our world. Jesus is not an impractical idealist; he is the practical realist.

I am certain that Jesus understood the difficulty inherent in the act of loving one's enemy. He never joined the ranks of those who talk glibly about the easiness of the moral life. He realized that every genuine expression of love grows out of a consistent and total surrender to God. So when Jesus said "Love your enemy," he was not unmindful of its stringent qualities. Yet he meant every word of it. Our responsibility as Christians is to discover the meaning of this command and seek passionately to live it out in our daily lives.

I

Let us be practical and ask the question, *How do we love our enemies?*

First, we must develop and maintain the capacity to forgive. He who is devoid of the power to forgive is devoid of the power to love. It is impossible even to begin the act of loving one's enemies without the prior acceptance of the necessity, over and over again, of forgiving those who inflict evil and injury upon us. It is also necessary to realize that the forgiving act must always be initiated by the person who has been wronged, the victim of some great hurt, the recipient of some tortuous injustice, the absorber of some terrible act of oppression. The wrongdoer may request forgiveness. He may come to himself, and, like the prodigal son, move up some dusty road, his heart palpitating with the desire for forgiveness. But only the injured neighbour, the loving father back home, can really pour out the warm waters of forgiveness.

Forgiveness does not mean ignoring what has been done or putting a false label on an evil act. It means, rather, that the evil act no longer remains as a barrier to the relationship. Forgiveness is a catalyst creating the atmosphere necessary for a fresh start and a new beginning. It is the lifting of a burden or the cancelling of a debt. The words "I will forgive you, but I'll never forget what you've done" never explain the real nature of forgiveness. Certainly one can never forget, if that means erasing it totally from his mind. But when we forgive, we forget in the sense that the evil deed is no longer a mental block impeding a new relationship. Likewise, we can never say, "I will forgive you, but I won't have anything further to do with you." Forgiveness means reconciliation, a coming together again. Without this, no man can love his enemies. The degree to which we are able to forgive determines the degree to which we are able to love our enemies.

Second, we must recognize that the evil deed of the enemy-neighbour, the thing that hurts, never quite expresses all that he is. An element of goodness may be found even in our worst enemy. Each of us is something of a schizophrenic personality, tragically divided against ourselves. A persistent civil war rages within all of our lives. Something within us causes us to lament with Ovid, the Latin poet, "I see and approve the better things, but follow worse," or to agree with Plato that human personality is like a charioteer having two headstrong horses, each wanting to go in a different direction, or to repeat with the Apostle Paul, "The good that I would I do not: but the evil which I would not, that I do."

This simply means that there is some good in the worst of us and some evil in the best of us. When we discover this, we are less prone to hate our enemies. When we look beneath the surface, beneath the impulsive evil deed, we see within our enemy-neighbour a measure of goodness and know that the viciousness and evilness of his acts are not quite representative of all that he is. We see him in a new light. We recognize that his hate grows out of fear, pride, ignorance, prejudice, and misunderstanding, but in spite of this, we know God's image is ineffably etched in his being. Then we love our enemies by realizing that they are not totally bad and that they are not beyond the reach of God's redemptive love.

Third, we must not seek to defeat or humiliate the enemy but to win his friendship and understanding. At times we are able to humiliate our worst enemy. Inevitably, his weak moments come and we are able to thrust in his side the spear of defeat. But this we must not do. Every word and deed must contribute to an understanding with the enemy and release those vast reservoirs of goodwill which have been blocked by impenetrable walls of hate.

The meaning of love is not to be confused with some sentimental outpouring. Love is something much deeper than emotional bosh. Perhaps the Greek language can clear our confusion at this point. In the Greek New Testament are three words for love. The word *eros* is a sort of aesthetic or romantic love. In the Platonic dialogues *eros* is a yearning of the soul for the realm of the divine. The second word is *philia*, a reciprocal love and the intimate affection and friendship between friends. We love those whom we like, and we love because we are loved. The third word is *agape*, understanding and creative, redemptive goodwill for all men. An overflowing love which seeks nothing in return, *agape* is the love of God operating in the human heart. At this level, we love men not because we like them, nor because their ways appeal to us, nor even because they possess some type of divine spark; we love every man because God loves him. At this level, we love the person who does an evil deed, although we hate the deed that he does.

Now we can see what Jesus meant when he said, "Love your enemies." We should be happy that he did not say, "Like your enemies." It is almost impossible to like some people. "Like" is a sentimental and affectionate word. How can we be affectionate toward a person whose avowed aim is to crush our very being and place innumerable stumbling blocks in our path? How can we like a person who is threatening our children and bombing our homes? That is impossible. But Jesus recognized that *love* is greater than *like*. When Jesus bids us to love our enemies, he is speaking neither of *eros* nor *philia*; he is speaking of *agape*, understanding and creative, redemptive goodwill for all men. Only by following this way and responding with this type of love are we able to be children of our Father who is in heaven.

II

Let us move now from the practical *how* to the theoretical *why*: *Why should we love our enemies?* The first reason is fairly obvious. Returning hate for hate multiplies hate, adding deeper darkness to a night already devoid of stars. Darkness cannot drive out darkness; only light can do that. Hate cannot drive out hate; only love can do that. Hate multiplies hate, violence multiplies violence, and toughness multiplies toughness in a descending spiral of destruction. So when Jesus says "Love your enemies," he is setting forth a profound and ultimately inescapable admonition. Have we not come to such an impasse in the modern world that we must love our enemies—or else? The chain reaction of evil—hate begetting hate, wars producing more wars—must be broken, or we shall be plunged into the dark abyss of annihilation.

Another reason why we must love our enemies is that hate scars the soul and distorts the personality. Mindful that hate is an evil and dangerous force, we too often think of what it does to the person hated. This is understandable, for hate brings irreparable damage to its victims. We have seen its ugly consequences in the ignominious deaths brought to six million Jews by a hate-obsessed madman named Hitler, in the unspeakable violence inflicted upon Negroes by bloodthirsty mobs, in the dark horrors of war, and in the terrible indignities and injustices perpetrated against millions of God's children by unconscionable oppressors.

But there is another side which we must never overlook. Hate is just as injurious to the person who hates. Like an unchecked cancer, hate corrodes the personality and eats away its vital unity. Hate destroys a man's sense of values and his objectivity. It causes him to describe the beautiful as ugly and the ugly as beautiful, and to confuse the true with the false and the false with the true.

Dr. E. Franklin Frazier, in an interesting essay entitled "The Pathology of Race Prejudice," included several examples of white persons who were normal, amiable, and congenial in their day-to-day relationships with other white persons but when they were challenged to think of Negroes as equals or even to discuss the question of racial injustice, they reacted with unbelievable irrationality and an abnormal unbalance. This happens when hate lingers in our minds. Psychiatrists report that many of the strange things that happen in the subconscious, many of our inner conflicts, are rooted in hate. They say, "Love or perish." Modern psychology recognizes what Jesus taught centuries ago: hate divides the personality and love in an amazing and inexorable way unites it.

A third reason why we should love our enemies is that love is the only force capable of transforming an enemy into a friend. We never get rid of an enemy by meeting hate with hate; we get rid of an enemy by getting rid of enmity. By its very nature, hate destroys and tears down; by its very nature, love creates and builds up. Love transforms with redemptive power.

Lincoln tried love and left for all history a magnificent drama of reconciliation. When he was campaigning for the presidency one of his arch-enemies was a man named Stanton. For some reason Stanton hated Lincoln. He used every ounce of his energy to degrade him in the eyes of the public. So deep rooted was Stanton's hate for Lincoln that he uttered unkind words about his physical appearance, and sought to embarrass him at every point with the bitterest diatribes. But in spite of this Lincoln was elected President of the United States. Then came the period when he had to select his cabinet which would consist of the persons who would be his most intimate associates in implementing his programme. He started choosing men here and there for the various secretaryships. The day finally came for Lincoln to select a man to fill the all-important post of Secretary of War. Can you imagine whom Lincoln chose to fill this post? None other than the man named Stanton. There was an immediate uproar in the inner circle when the news began to spread. Adviser after adviser was heard saying, "Mr. President, you are making a mistake. Do you know this man Stanton? Are you familiar with all of the ugly things he said about you? He is your enemy. He will seek to sabotage your programme. Have you thought this through, Mr. President?" Mr. Lincoln's answer was terse and to the point: "Yes, I know Mr. Stanton. I am aware of all the terrible things he has said about me. But after looking over the nation, I find he is the best man for the job." So Stanton became Abraham Lincoln's Secretary of War and rendered an invaluable service to his nation and his President. Not many years later Lincoln was assassinated. Many laudable things were said about him. Even today millions of people still adore him as the greatest of all Americans. H. G. Wells selected him as one of the six great men of history. But of all the great statements made about Abraham Lincoln, the words of Stanton remain among the greatest. Standing near the dead body of the man he once hated, Stanton referred to him as one of the greatest men that ever lived and said "he now belongs to the ages." If Lincoln had hated Stanton both men would have gone to their graves as bitter enemies. But through the power of love Lincoln transformed an enemy into a friend. It was this same attitude that made it possible for Lincoln to speak a kind word about the South during the Civil War when feeling was most bitter. Asked by a shocked bystander how he could do this, Lincoln said, "Madam, do I not destroy my enemies when I make them my friends?" This is the power of redemptive love.

We must hasten to say that these are not the ultimate reasons why we should love our enemies. An even more basic reason why we are commanded to love is expressed explicitly in Jesus' words, "Love your enemies . . . *that ye may be children of your Father which is in heaven.*" We are called to this difficult task in order to realize a unique relationship with God. We are potential sons of God. Through love that potentiality becomes actuality. We must love our enemies, because only by loving them can we know God and experience the beauty of his holiness.

The relevance of what I have said to the crisis in race relations should be readily apparent. There will be no permanent solution to the race problem until oppressed men develop the capacity to love their enemies. The darkness of racial injustice will be dispelled only by the light of forgiving love. For more than three centuries American Negroes have been battered by the iron rod of oppression, frustrated by day and bewildered by night by unbearable injustice, and burdened with the ugly weight of discrimination. Forced to live with these shameful conditions, we are tempted to become bitter and to retaliate with a corresponding hate. But if this happens, the new order we seek will be little more than a duplicate of the old order. We must in strength and humility meet hate with love.

Of course, this is not *practical*. Life is a matter of getting even, of hitting back, of dog eat dog. Am I saying that Jesus commands us to love those who hurt and oppress us? Do I sound like most preachers—idealistic and impractical? Maybe in some distant Utopia, you say, that idea will work, but not in the hard, cold world in which we live.

My friends, we have followed the so-called practical way for too long a time now, and it has led inexorably to deeper confusion and chaos. Time is cluttered with the wreckage of communities which surrendered to hatred and violence. For the salvation of our nation and the salvation of mankind, we must follow another way. This does not mean that we abandon our righteous efforts. With every ounce of our energy we must continue to rid this nation of the incubus of segregation. But we shall not in the process relinquish our privilege and our obligation to love. While abhorring segregation, we shall love the segregationist. This is the only way to create the beloved community.

To our most bitter opponents we say: "We shall match your capacity to inflict suffering by our capacity to endure suffering. We shall meet your physical force with soul force. Do to us what you will, and we shall continue to love you. We cannot in all good conscience obey your unjust laws, because non-co-operation with evil is as much a moral obligation as is co-operation with good. Throw us in jail, and we shall still love you. Send your hooded perpetrators of violence into our community at the midnight hour and beat us and leave us half dead, and we shall still love you. But be ye assured that we will wear you down by our capacity to suffer. One day we shall win freedom, but not only for ourselves. We shall so appeal to your heart and conscience that we shall win *you* in the process, and our victory will be a double victory."

Love is the most durable power in the world. This creative force, so beautifully exemplified in the life of our Christ, is the most potent instrument available in mankind's quest for peace and security. Napoleon Bonaparte, the great military genius, looking back over his years of conquest, is reported to have said: "Alexander, Caesar, Charlemagne and I have built great empires. But upon what did they depend? They depended on force. But centuries ago Jesus started an empire that was built on love, and even to this day millions will die for him." Who can doubt the veracity of these words. The great military leaders of the past have gone, and their empires have crumbled and burned to ashes. But the empire of Jesus, built solidly and majestically on the foundation of love, is still growing. It started with a small group of dedicated men, who, through the inspiration of their Lord, were able to shake the hinges from the gates of the Roman Empire, and carry the gospel into all the world. Today the vast earthly kingdom of Christ numbers more than 900,000,000 and covers every land and tribe. Today we hear again the promise of victory:

> Jesus shall reign where'er the sun
> Does his successive journeys run;
> His kingdom stretch from shore to shore,
> Till moon shall wax and wane no more.

Another choir joyously responds:

> In Christ there is no East or West,
> In Him no South or North,
> But one great Fellowship of Love
> Throughout the whole wide earth.

Jesus is eternally right. History is replete with the bleached bones of nations that refused to listen to him. May we in the twentieth century hear and follow his words—before it is too late. May we solemnly realize that we shall never be true sons of our heavenly Father until we love our enemies and pray for those who persecute us.

CHAPTER SIX

A knock at midnight

*Which of you who has a friend will go
to him at midnight and say to him,
"Friend, lend me three loaves; for a
friend of mine has arrived on a journey,
and I have nothing to set before him"?*
                                        Luke 11:5-6, RSV

Although this parable is concerned with the power of persistent prayer, it may also serve as a basis for our thought concerning many contemporary problems and the role of the church in grappling with them. It is midnight in the parable; it is also midnight in our world, and the darkness is so deep that we can hardly see which way to turn.

I

It is midnight within the social order. On the international horizon nations are engaged in a colossal and bitter contest for supremacy. Two world wars have been fought within a generation, and the clouds of another war are dangerously low. Man now has atomic and nuclear weapons that could within seconds completely destroy the major cities of the world. Yet the arms race continues and nuclear tests still explode in the atmosphere, with the grim prospect that the very air we breathe will be poisoned by radioactive fallout. Will these circumstances and weapons bring the annihilation of the human race?

When confronted by midnight in the social order we have in the past turned to science for help. And little wonder! On so many occasions science has saved us. When we were in the midnight of physical limitation and material inconvenience, science lifted us to the bright morning of physical and material comfort. When we were in the midnight of crippling ignorance and superstition, science brought us to the daybreak of the free and open mind. When we were in the midnight of dread plagues and diseases, science, through surgery, sanitation, and the wonder drugs, ushered in the bright day of physical health, thereby prolonging our lives and making for greater security and physical well-being. How naturally we turn to science in a day when the problems of the world are so ghastly and ominous.

But alas! science cannot now rescue us, for even the scientist is lost in the terrible midnight of our age. Indeed, science gave us the very instruments that threaten to bring universal suicide. So modern man faces a dreary and frightening midnight in the social order.

This midnight in man's external collective life is paralleled by midnight in his internal individual life. It is midnight within the psychological order. Everywhere paralyzing fears harrow people by day and haunt them by night. Deep clouds of anxiety and depression are suspended in our mental skies. More people are emotionally disturbed today than at any other time of human history. The psychopathic wards of our hospitals are crowded, and the most popular psychologists today are the psychoanalysts. Bestsellers in psychology are books such as *Man Against Himself*, *The Neurotic Personality of Our Times*, and *Modern Man in Search of a Soul*. Bestsellers in religion are such books as *Peace of Mind* and *Peace of Soul*. The popular clergyman preaches soothing sermons on "How to Be Happy" and "How to Relax." Some have been tempted to revise Jesus' command to read, "Go ye into all the world, keep your blood pressure down, and, lo, I will make you a well-adjusted personality." All of this is indicative that it is midnight within the inner lives of men and women.

It is also midnight within the moral order. At midnight

colours lose their distinctiveness and become a sullen shade of grey. Moral principles have lost their distinctiveness. For modern man, absolute right and absolute wrong are a matter of what the majority is doing. Right and wrong are relative to likes and dislikes and the customs of a particular community. We have unconsciously applied Einstein's theory of relativity, which properly described the physical universe, to the moral and ethical realm.

Midnight is the hour when men desperately seek to obey the eleventh commandment, "Thou shalt not get caught." According to the ethic of midnight, the cardinal sin is to be caught and the cardinal virtue is to get by. It is all right to lie, but one must lie with real finesse. It is all right to steal, if one is so dignified that, if caught, the charge becomes embezzlement, not robbery. It is permissible even to hate, if one so dresses his hating in the garments of love that hating appears to be loving. The Darwinian concept of the survival of the fittest has been substituted by a philosophy of the survival of the slickest. This mentality has brought a tragic breakdown of moral standards, and the midnight of moral degeneration deepens.

II

As in the parable, so in our world today, the deep darkness of midnight is interrupted by the sound of a knock. On the door of the church millions of people knock. In this country the roll of church members is longer than ever before. More than one hundred and fifteen million people are at least paper members of some church or synagogue. This represents an increase of 100 per cent since 1929, although the population has increased by only 31 per cent.

Visitors to Soviet Russia, whose official policy is atheistic, report that the churches in that nation not only are crowded, but that attendance continues to grow. Harrison Salisbury, in an article in *The New York Times*, states that Communist officials are disturbed that so many young people express a growing interest in the church and religion. After forty years of the most vigorous efforts to suppress religion, the hierarchy of the Communist party now faces the inescapable fact that millions of people are knocking on the door of the church.

This numerical growth should not be overemphasized. We must not be tempted to confuse spiritual power and large numbers. Jumboism, as someone has called it, is an utterly fallacious standard for measuring positive power. An increase in quantity does not automatically bring an increase in quality. A larger membership does not necessarily represent a correspondingly increased commitment to Christ. Almost always the creative, dedicated minority has made the world better. But although a numerical growth in church membership does not necessarily reflect a concomitant increase in ethical commitment, millions of people do feel that the church provides an answer to the deep confusion that encompasses their lives. It is still the one familiar landmark where the weary traveller by midnight comes. It is the one house which stands where it has always stood, the house to which the man travelling at midnight either comes or refuses to come. Some decide not to come. But the many who come and knock are desperately seeking a little bread to tide them over.

The traveller asks for three loaves of bread. He wants the bread of faith. In a generation of so many colossal disappointments, men have lost faith in God, faith in man, and faith in the future. Many feel as did William Wilberforce, who in 1801 said, "I dare not marry—the future is so unsettled," or as did William Pitt, who in 1806 said, "There is scarcely anything round us but ruin and despair." In the midst of staggering disillusionment, many cry for the bread of faith.

There is also a deep longing for the bread of hope. In the early years of this century many people did not hunger for this bread. The days of the first telephones, automobiles, and aeroplanes gave them a radiant optimism. They worshipped at the shrine of inevitable progress. They believed that every new scientific achievement lifted man to higher levels of perfection. But then a series of tragic developments, revealing the selfishness and corruption of man, illustrated with frightening clarity the truth of Lord Acton's dictum, "Power tends to corrupt and absolute power corrupts absolutely." This awful discovery led to one of the most colossal breakdowns of optimism in history. For so many people, young and old, the light of hope went out, and they roamed wearily in the dark chambers of pessimism. Many concluded that life has no meaning. Some agreed with the philosopher Schopenhauer that life is an endless pain with a painful end, and that life is a tragicomedy played over and over again with only slight changes in costume and scenery. Others cried out with Shakespeare's Macbeth that life

<blockquote>
is a tale
Told by an idiot, full of sound and fury,
Signifying nothing.
</blockquote>

But even in the inevitable moments when all seems hopeless, men know that without hope they cannot really live, and in agonizing desperation they cry for the bread of hope.

And there is the deep longing for the bread of love. Everybody wishes to love and to be loved. He who feels that he is not loved feels that he does not count. Much has happened in the modern world to make men feel that they do not belong. Living in a world which has become oppressively impersonal, many of us have come to feel that we are little more than numbers. Ralph Borsodi in an arresting picture of a world wherein numbers have replaced persons writes that the modern mother is often maternity case No. 8434 and her child, after being fingerprinted and footprinted, becomes No. 8003, and that a funeral in a large city is an event in Parlour B with Class B flowers and decorations at which Preacher No. 14 officiates and Musician No. 84 sings Selection No. 174. Bewildered by this tendency to reduce man to a card in a vast index, man desperately searches for the bread of love.

III

When the man in the parable knocked on his friend's door and asked for the three loaves of bread, he received the impatient retort, "Do not bother me; the door is now shut, and my children are with me in bed; I cannot get up and give you anything." How often have men experienced a similar disappointment when at midnight they knock on the door of the church. Millions of Africans, patiently knocking on the door of the Christian church where they seek the bread of social justice, have either been altogether ignored or told to wait until later, which almost always means never. Millions of American Negroes, starving for the want of the bread of freedom, have knocked again and again on the door of so-called white churches, but they have usually been greeted by a cold indifference or a blatant hypocrisy. Even the white religious leaders, who have a heartfelt desire to open the door and provide the bread, are often more cautious than courageous and more prone to follow the expedient than the ethical path. One of the shameful tragedies of history is that the very institution which should remove man from the midnight of racial segregation participates in creating and perpetuating the midnight.

In the terrible midnight of war men have knocked on the door of the church to ask for the bread of peace, but the church has often disappointed them. What more pathetically reveals the irrelevancy of the church in present-day world affairs than its witness regarding war? In a world gone mad with arms buildups, chauvinistic passions, and imperialistic exploitation, the church has either endorsed these activities or remained appallingly silent. During the last two world wars, national churches even functioned as the ready lackeys of the state, sprinkling holy water upon the battleships and joining the mighty armies in singing, "Praise the Lord and pass the ammunition." A weary world, pleading desperately for peace, has often found the church morally sanctioning war.

And those who have gone to the church to seek the bread of. economic justice have been left in the frustrating midnight of economic privation. In many instances the church has so aligned itself with the privileged classes and so defended the status quo that it has been unwilling to answer the knock at midnight. The Greek Church in Russia allied itself with the status quo and became so inextricably bound to the despotic czarist regime that it became impossible to be rid of the corrupt political and social system without being rid of the church. Such is the fate of every ecclesiastical organization that allies itself with things-as-they-are.

The church must be reminded that it is not the master or the servant of the state, but rather the conscience of the state. It must be the guide and the critic of the state, and never its tool. If the church does not recapture its prophetic zeal, it will become an irrelevant social club without moral or spiritual authority. If the church does not participate actively in the struggle for peace and for economic and racial justice, it will forfeit the loyalty of millions and cause men everywhere to say that it has atrophied its will. But if the church will free itself from the shackles of a deadening status quo, and, recovering its great historic mission, will speak and act fearlessly and insistently in terms of justice and peace, it will enkindle the imagination of mankind and fire the souls of men, imbuing them with a glowing and ardent love for truth, justice, and peace. Men far and near will know the church as a great fellowship of love that provides light and bread for lonely travellers at midnight.

While speaking of the laxity of the church, I must not overlook the fact that the so-called Negro church has also left men disappointed at midnight. I say so-called Negro church because ideally there can be no Negro or white church. It is to their everlasting shame that white Christians developed a system of racial segregation within the church, and inflicted so many indignities upon its Negro worshippers that they had to organize their own churches.

Two types of Negro churches have failed to provide bread. One burns with emotionalism, and the other freezes with classism. The former, reducing worship to entertainment, places more emphasis on volume than on content and confuses spirituality with muscularity. The danger in such a church is that the members may have more religion in their hands and feet than in their hearts and souls. At midnight this type of church has neither the vitality nor the relevant gospel to feed hungry souls.

The other type of Negro church that feeds no midnight traveller has developed a class system and boasts of its dignity, its membership of professional people, and its exclusiveness. In such a church the worship service is cold and meaningless, the music dull and uninspiring, and the sermon little more than a homily on current events. If the pastor says too much about Jesus Christ, the members feel that he is robbing the pulpit of dignity. If the choir sings a Negro spiritual, the members claim an affront to their class status. This type of church tragically fails to recognize that worship at its best is a social experience in which people from all levels of life come together to affirm their oneness and unity under God. At midnight men are altogether ignored because of their limited education, or they are given bread that has been hardened by the winter of morbid class consciousness.

IV

In the parable we notice that after the man's initial disappointment, he continued to knock on his friend's door. Because of his importunity—his persistence—he finally persuaded his friend to open the door. Many men continue to knock on the door of the church at midnight, even after the church has so bitterly disappointed them, because they know the bread of life is there. The church today is challenged to proclaim God's Son, Jesus Christ, to be the hope of men in all of their complex personal and social problems. Many will continue to come in quest of answers to life's problems. Many young people who knock on the door are perplexed by the uncertainties of life, confused by daily disappointments, and disillusioned by the ambiguities of history. Some who come have been taken from their schools and careers and cast in the role of soldiers. We must provide them with the fresh bread of hope and imbue them with the conviction that God has the power to bring good out of evil. Some who come are tortured by a nagging guilt resulting from their wandering in the midnight of ethical relativism and their surrender to the doctrine of self-expression. We must lead them to Christ who will offer them the fresh bread of forgiveness. Some who knock are tormented by the fear of death as they move toward the evening of life. We must provide them with the bread of faith in immortality, so that they may realize that this earthly life is merely an embryonic prelude to a new awakening.

Midnight is a confusing hour when it is difficult to be faithful. The most inspiring word that the church may speak is that no midnight long remains. The weary traveller by midnight who asks for bread is really seeking the dawn. Our eternal message of hope is that dawn will come. Our slave foreparents realized this. They were never unmindful of the fact of midnight, for always there was the rawhide whip of the overseer and the auction block where families were torn asunder to remind them of its reality. When they thought of the agonizing darkness of midnight, they sang:

> Oh, nobody knows de trouble I've seen,
> Glory Hallelujah!
>
> Sometimes I'm up, sometimes I'm down,
> Oh, yes, Lord,
>
> Sometimes I'm almost to de groun',
> Oh, yes, Lord,
>
> Oh, nobody knows de trouble I've seen,
> Glory Hallelujah!

Encompassed by a staggering midnight but believing that morning would come, they sang:

> I'm so glad trouble don't last alway.
> O my Lord, O my Lord, what shall I do?

Their positive belief in the dawn was the growing edge of hope that kept the slaves faithful amid the most barren and tragic circumstances.

Faith in the dawn arises from the faith that God is good and just. When one believes this, he knows that the contradictions of life are neither final nor ultimate. He can walk through the dark night with the radiant conviction that all things work together for good for those that love God. Even the most starless midnight may herald the dawn of some great fulfilment.

At the beginning of the bus boycott in Montgomery, Alabama, we set up a voluntary car pool to get the people to and from their jobs. For eleven long months our car pool functioned extraordinarily well. Then Mayor Gayle introduced a resolution instructing the city's legal department to file such proceedings as it might deem proper to stop the operation of the car pool or any transportation system growing out of the bus boycott. A hearing was set for Tuesday, November 13, 1956.

At our regular weekly mass meeting, scheduled the night before the hearing, I had the responsibility of warning the people that the car pool would probably be enjoined. I knew that they had willingly suffered for nearly twelve months, but could we now ask them to walk back and forth to their jobs? And if not, would we be forced to admit that the protest had failed? For the first time I almost shrank from appearing before them.

When the evening came, I mustered sufficient courage to tell them the truth. I tried, however, to conclude on a note of hope. "We have moved all of these months," I said, "in the daring faith that God is with us in our struggle. The many experiences of days gone by have vindicated that faith in a marvellous way. Tonight we must believe that a way will be made out of no way." Yet I could feel the cold breeze of pessimism pass over the audience. The night was darker than a thousand midnights. The light of hope was about to fade and the lamp of faith to flicker.

A few hours later, before Judge Carter, the city argued that we were operating a "private enterprise" without a franchise. Our lawyers argued brilliantly that the car pool was a voluntary "share-a-ride" plan provided without profit as a service by Negro churches. It became obvious that Judge Carter would rule in favour of the city.

At noon, during a brief recess, I noticed an unusual commotion in the courtroom. Mayor Gayle was called to the back room. Several reporters moved excitedly in and out of the room. Momentarily a reporter came to the table where, as chief defendent, I sat with the lawyers. "Here is the decision that you have been waiting for," he said. "Read this release."

In anxiety and hope, I read these words: "The United States Supreme Court today unanimously ruled bus segregation unconstitutional in Montgomery, Alabama." My heart throbbed with an inexpressible joy. The darkest hour of our struggle had become the first hour of victory. Someone shouted from the back of the courtroom, "God Almighty has spoken from Washington!"

The dawn will come. Disappointment, sorrow, and despair are born at midnight, but morning follows. "Weeping may endure for a night," says the Psalmist, "but joy cometh in the morning." This faith adjourns the assemblies of hopelessness and brings new light into the dark chambers of pessimism.

CHAPTER SEVEN

The man who was a fool

*Thou fool, this night thy soul shall be
required of thee.*   Luke 12:20

I would like to share with you a dramatic little story that
is significantly relevant in its implications and profoundly
meaningful in its conclusions. It is the story of a man who
by all modern standards would be considered eminently successful. Yet Jesus called him a fool.

The central character in the drama is a "certain rich
man," whose farm yielded such heavy crops that he decided
to build new and larger barns, saying, "There will I bestow
all my fruits and my goods. And I will say to my soul, Soul,
thou hast much goods laid up for many years; take thine
ease, eat, drink, and be merry." But God said to him,
"Thou fool, this night thy soul shall be required of thee."
And it was so. At the height of his prosperity, he died.

Think of this man. If he lived in our community today,
he would be considered "a big shot." He would abound with
social prestige and community respectability. He would be
one of the privileged few in the economic power structure.
And yet a Galilean peasant had the audacity to call him a
fool.

Jesus did not call this man a fool merely because he possessed wealth. Jesus never made a sweeping indictment
against wealth. Rather, he condemned the misuse of wealth.
Money, like any other force such as electricity, is amoral
and can be used for either good or evil. It is true that

Jesus commanded the rich young ruler to "sell all," but in this instance, as Dr. George A. Buttrick has said, Jesus was prescribing individual surgery, not making a universal diagnosis. Nothing in wealth is inherently vicious, and nothing in poverty is inherently virtuous.

Jesus did not condemn this man because he had made money in a dishonest fashion. Apparently he acquired his wealth by hard work and the practical know-how and far-sighted vision of a good businessman. Why, then, was he a fool?

I

The rich man was a fool because he permitted the ends for which he lived to become confused with the means by which he lived. The economic structure of his life absorbed his destiny. Each of us lives in two realms, the internal and the external. The internal is that realm of spiritual ends expressed in art, literature, morals, and religion. The external is that complex of devices, techniques, mechanisms, and instrumentalities by means of which we live. These include the house we live in, the car we drive, the clothes we wear, the economic sources we acquire—the material stuff we must have to exist. There is always a danger that we will permit the means by which we live to replace the ends for which we live, the internal to become lost in the external. The rich man was a fool because he failed to keep a line of distinction between means and ends, between structure and destiny. His life was submerged in the rolling waters of his livelihood. This does not mean that the external in our lives is not important. We have both a privilege and a duty to seek the basic material necessities of life. Only an irrelevant religion fails to be concerned about man's economic well-being. Religion at its best realizes that the soul is crushed as long as the body is tortured with hunger pangs and harrowed with the need for shelter. Jesus realized that we need food, clothing, shelter, and economic security. He said in clear and concise terms: "Your Father knoweth what things ye have need of." But Jesus knew that man was more than a dog to be satisfied by a few economic bones. He realized that the internal of a man's life is as significant as the external. So he added, "Seek ye first the kingdom of God, and his righteousness; and all these things shall be added unto you." The tragedy of the rich man was that he sought the means first, and in the process the ends were swallowed in the means.

The richer this man became materially the poorer he became intellectually and spiritually. He may have been married, but he probably could not love his wife. It is possible that he gave her countless material gifts, but he could not give her that which she needed most, love and affection. He may have had children, but he probably did not appreciate them. He may have had the great books of the ages shelved neatly in his library, but he never read them. He may have had access to great music, but he did not listen. His eyes did not behold the majestic splendour of the skies. His ears were not attuned to the melodious sweetness of heavenly music. His mind was closed to the insights of poets, prophets, and philosophers. His title was justly merited —"Thou fool!"

II

The rich man was a fool because he failed to realize his dependence on others. His soliloquy contains approximately sixty words, yet "I" and "my" occur twelve times. He has said "I" and "my" so often that he had lost the capacity to say "we" and "our." A victim of the cancerous disease of egotism, he failed to realize that wealth always comes as a result of the commonwealth. He talked as though he could plough the fields and build the barns alone. He failed to realize that he was an heir of a vast treasury of ideas and labour to which both the living and the dead had contributed. When an individual or a nation overlooks this interdependence, we find a tragic foolishness.

We can clearly see the meaning of this parable for the present world crisis. Our nation's productive machinery constantly brings forth such an abundance of food that we must build larger barns and spend more than a million dollars daily to store our surplus. Year after year we ask, "What shall I do, because I have no room where to bestow my fruits?" I have seen an answer in the faces of millions of poverty-stricken men and women in Asia, Africa, and South America. I have seen an answer in the appalling poverty in the Mississippi Delta and the tragic insecurity of the unemployed in large industrial cities of the North. What can we do? The answer is simple: feed the poor, clothe the naked, and heal the sick. Where can we store our goods? Again the answer is simple: we can store our surplus food free of charge in the shrivelled stomachs of the millions of God's children who go to bed hungry at night. We can use our vast resources of wealth to wipe poverty from the earth.

All of this tells us something basic about the interdependence of men and nations. Whether we realize it or not, each of us is eternally "in the red." We are everlasting debtors to known and unknown men and women. We do not finish breakfast without being dependent on more than half of the world. When we arise in the morning, we go into the bathroom where we reach for a sponge which is provided for us by a Pacific Islander. We reach for soap that is created for us by a Frenchman. The towel is provided by a Turk. Then at the table we drink coffee which is provided for us by a South American, or tea by a Chinese, or cocoa by a West African. Before we leave for our jobs we are beholden to more than half the world.

In a real sense, all life is interrelated. All men are caught in an inescapable network of mutuality, tied in a single garment of destiny. Whatever affects one directly affects all indirectly. I can never be what I ought to be until you are what you ought to be, and you can never be what you ought to be until I am what I ought to be. This is the interrelated structure of reality.

The rich man tragically failed to realize this. He thought

that he could live and grow in his little self-centred world. He was an individualist gone wild. Indeed, he was an eternal fool!

III

Jesus called the rich man a fool because he failed to realize his dependence on God. He talked as though he unfolded the seasons and provided the fertility of the soil, controlled the rising and the setting of the sun, and regulated the natural processes that produce the rain and the dew. He had an unconscious feeling that he was the Creator, not a creature.

This man-centred foolishness has had a long and ofttimes disastrous reign in the history of mankind. Sometimes it is theoretically expressed in the doctrine of materialism, which contends that reality may be explained in terms of matter in motion, that life is "a physiological process with a physiological meaning," that man is a transient accident of protons and electrons travelling blind, that thought is a temporary product of grey matter, and that the events of history are an interaction of matter and motion operating by the principle of necessity. Having no place for God or for eternal ideas, materialism is opposed to both theism and idealism.

This materialistic philosophy leads inevitably into a dead-end street in an intellectually senseless world. To believe that human personality is the result of the fortuitous interplay of atoms and electrons is as absurd as to believe that a monkey by hitting typewriter keys at random will eventually produce a Shakespearean play. Sheer magic! It is much more sensible to say with Sir James Jeans, the physicist, that "the universe seems to be nearer to a great thought than to a great machine," or with Arthur Balfour, the philosopher, that "we now know too much about matter to be materialists." Materialism is a weak flame that is blown out by the breath of mature thinking.

Another attempt to make God irrelevant is found in nontheistic humanism, a philosophy that deifies man by affirming that humanity is God. Man is the measure of all things. Many modern men who have embraced this philosophy contend, as did Rousseau, that human nature is essentially good. Evil is to be found only in institutions, and if poverty and ignorance were to be removed everything would be all right. The twentieth century opened with such a glowing optimism. Men believed that civilization was evolving toward an earthly paradise. Herbert Spencer skilfully moulded the Darwinian theory of evolution into the heady idea of automatic progress. Men became convinced that there is a sociological law of progress which is as valid as the physical law of gravitation.

Possessed of this spirit of optimism, modern man broke into the storehouse of nature and emerged with many scientific insights and technological developments that completely revolutionized the earth. The achievements of science have been marvellous, tangible, and concrete.

Witnessing the amazing advances of science, modern man exclaimed:

> Science is my shepherd; I shall not want.
> It maketh me to lie down in green pastures:
> It leadeth me beside the still waters.
> It restoreth my soul. . . .
> I will fear no evil: for science is with me;
> Its rod and its staff they comfort me.

Man's aspirations no longer turned Godward and heavenward. Rather, man's thoughts were confined to man and earth. And man offered a strange parody on the Lord's Prayer: "Our brethren which art upon the earth, Hallowed be our name. Our kingdom come. Our will be done on earth, for there is no heaven." Those who formerly turned to God to find solutions for their problems turned to science and technology, convinced that they now possessed the instruments needed to usher in the new society.

Then came the explosion of this myth. It climaxed in the horrors of Nagasaki and Hiroshima and in the fierce fury of fifty-megaton bombs. Now we have come to see that science can give us only physical power, which, if not controlled by spiritual power, will lead inevitably to cosmic doom. The words of Alfred the Great are still true: "Power is never a good unless he be good that has it." We need something more spiritually sustaining and morally controlling than science. It is an instrument which, under the power of God's spirit, may lead man to greater heights of physical security, but apart from God's spirit, science is a deadly weapon that will lead only to deeper chaos. Why fool ourselves about automatic progress and the ability of man to save himself? We must lift up our minds and eyes unto the hills from whence cometh our true help. Then, and only then, will the advances of modern science be a blessing rather than a curse.

Without dependence on God our efforts turn to ashes and our sunrises into darkest night. Unless his spirit pervades our lives, we find only what G. K. Chesterton called "cures that don't cure, blessings that don't bless, and solutions that don't solve." "God is our refuge and strength, a very present help in trouble."

Unfortunately, the rich man did not realize this. He, like many men of the twentieth century, became so involved in big affairs and small trivialities that he forgot God. He gave the finite infinite significance and elevated a preliminary concern to ultimate standing.

After the rich man had accumulated his vast resources of wealth—at the moment when his stocks were accruing the greatest interest and his palatial home was the talk of the town—he came to that experience which is the irreducible common denominator of all men, death. The fact that he died at this particular time adds verve and drama to the story, but the essential truth of the parable would have remained the same had he lived to be as old as Methuselah. Even if he had not died physically, he was already dead spiritually. The cessation of breathing was a belated announcement of an earlier death. He died when he failed to keep a line of distinction between the means by which he lived and the ends for which he lived and when he failed to recognize his dependence on others and on God.

May it not be that the "certain rich man" is Western civilization? Rich in goods and material resources, our

standards of success are almost inextricably bound to the
lust for acquisition. The means by which we live are marvellous indeed. And yet something is missing. We have
learned to fly the air like birds and swim the sea like fish,
but we have not learned the simple art of living together
as brothers. Our abundance has brought us neither peace
of mind nor serenity of spirit. An Oriental writer has por-
trayed our dilemma in candid terms:

> You call your thousand material devices "labour-saving
> machinery," yet you are forever "busy." With the multiply-
> ing of your machinery you grow increasingly fatigued,
> anxious, nervous, dissatisfied. Whatever you have, you want
> more; and wherever you are you want to go somewhere
> else. You have a machine to dig the raw material for
> you . . . , a machine to manufacture [it] . . . , a machine
> to transport [it] . . . , a machine to sweep and dust, one
> to carry messages, one to write, one to talk, one to sing,
> one to play at the theatre, one to vote, one to sew, . . . and
> a hundred others to do a hundred other things for you,
> and still you are the most nervously busy man in the
> world . . . your devices are neither time-saving nor soul-
> saving machinery. They are so many sharp spurs which
> urge you on to invent more machinery and to do more
> business.

This is poignantly true and tells us something about Western
civilization that cannot be cast aside as a prejudiced charge
by an Oriental thinker who is jealous of Occidental prosperity. We cannot escape the indictment. The means by
which we live have outdistanced the ends for which we
live. Our scientific power has outrun our spiritual power.
We have guided missiles and misguided man. Like the rich
man of old, we have foolishly minimized the internal of
our lives and maximized the external. We have absorbed
life in livelihood. We will not find peace in our generation
until we learn anew that "a man's life consisteth not in the
abundance of the things which he possesseth," but in those
inner treasuries of the spirit which "no thief approacheth,
neither moth corrupteth."

Our hope for creative living lies in our ability to reestablish the spiritual ends of our lives in personal character and social justice. Without this spiritual and moral reawakening we shall destroy ourselves in the misuse of our own instruments. Our generation cannot escape the question of our Lord: What shall it profit a man, if he gain the whole world of externals—aeroplanes, electric lights, automobiles, and colour television—and lose the internal—his own soul?

CHAPTER EIGHT

The death of evil upon the seashore

And Israel saw the Egyptians dead upon the sea shore.   Exodus 14:30

Is anything more obvious than the presence of evil in the universe? Its nagging, prehensile tentacles project into every level of human existence. We may debate the origin of evil, but only a victim of superficial optimism would debate its reality. Evil is stark, grim, and colossally real.

Affirming the reality of evil in unmistakable terms, the Bible symbolically pictures the conniving work of a serpent which injects discord into the harmonious symphony of life in a garden, prophetically denounces callous injustice and ugly hypocrisy, and dramatically portrays a misguided mob hanging the world's most precious Person on a cross between two thieves. Crystal clear is the biblical perception of evil. Nor was Jesus unmindful of the reality of evil. Although he never offered a theological explanation of the origin of evil, he never attempted to explain it away. In the parable of the tares, Jesus says that tares are tares, not illusions or errors of the mortal mind. Real weeds disrupt the orderly growth of stately wheat. Whether sown by Satan or by man's misuse of his own freedom, the tares are always poisonous and deadly. Concerning the choking weeds, Jesus says in substance, "I do not attempt to explain their origin, but they are the work of an enemy." He recognized that the force of evil was as real as the force of good.

Within the wide arena of everyday life we see evil in

all of its ugly dimensions. We see it expressed in tragic lust and inordinate selfishness. We see it in high places where men are willing to sacrifice truth on the altars of their self-interest. We see it in imperialistic nations crushing other people with the battering rams of social injustice. We see it clothed in the garments of calamitous wars which leave men and nations morally and physically bankrupt.

In a sense, the history of man is the story of the struggle between good and evil. All of the great religions have recognized a tension at the very core of the universe. Hinduism, for instance, calls this tension a conflict between illusion and reality; Zoroastrianism, a conflict between the god of light and the god of darkness; and traditional Judaism and Christianity, a conflict between God and Satan. Each realizes that in the midst of the upward thrust of goodness there is the downward pull of evil.

Christianity clearly affirms that in the long struggle between good and evil, good eventually will emerge as victor. Evil is ultimately doomed by the powerful, inexorable forces of good. Good Friday must give way to the triumphant music of Easter. Degrading tares choke the sprouting necks of growing wheat for a season, but when the harvest is gleaned the evil tares will be separated from the good wheat. Caesar occupied a palace and Christ a cross, but the same Christ so split history into A.D. and B.C. that even the reign of Caesar was subsequently dated by his name. Long ago biblical religion recognized what William Cullen Bryant affirmed, "Truth crushed to earth will rise again," and what Thomas Carlyle wrote, "No lie you can speak or act but it will come, after longer or shorter circulation, like a bill drawn on Nature's Reality, and be presented there for payment—with the answer, No effects."

I

A graphic example of this truth is found in the early history of the Hebrew people. When the children of Israel were held under the gripping yoke of Egyptian slavery, Egypt symbolized evil in the form of humiliating oppression, ungodly exploitation, and crushing domination, and the Israelites symbolized goodness in the form of devotion and dedication to the God of Abraham, Isaac, and Jacob. Egypt struggled to maintain her oppressive yoke, and Israel struggled to gain freedom. Pharaoh stubbornly refused to respond to the cry of Moses, even when plague after plague threatened his domain. This tells us something about evil that we must never forget, namely that evil is recalcitrant and determined, and never voluntarily relinquishes its hold short of a persistent, almost fanatical resistance. But there is a checkpoint in the universe: evil cannot permanently organize itself. So after a long and trying struggle, the Israelites, through the providence of God, crossed the Red Sea. But like the old guard that never surrenders, the Egyptians, in a desperate attempt to prevent the Israelites from escaping, had their armies go in the Red Sea behind them. As soon as the Egyptians got into the dried-up sea the parted waters swept back upon them, and the turbulence and momentum of the tidal waves soon drowned all of them. When the Israelites looked back, all they could see was here and there a poor drowned body beaten upon the seashore. For the Israelites, this was a great moment. It was the end of a frightful period in their history. It was a joyous daybreak that had come to end the long night of their captivity. The meaning of this story is not found in the drowning of Egyptian soldiers, for no one should rejoice at the death or defeat of a human being. Rather, this story symbolizes the death of evil and of inhuman oppression and unjust exploitation.

The death of the Egyptians upon the seashore is a vivid reminder that something in the very nature of the universe assists goodness in its perennial struggle with evil. The New Testament rightly declares: "No chastening for the present seemeth to be joyous, but grievous: *nevertheless afterward* it yieldeth the peaceable fruit of righteousness." Pharaoh exploits the children of Israel—*nevertheless afterward*! Pilate yields to the crowd which crucifies Christ—*nevertheless afterward*! The early Christians are thrown to the lions and

carried to the chopping blocks—*nevertheless afterward*!
Something in this universe justifies Shakespeare in saying:

> There's a divinity that shapes our ends,
> Rough-hew them how we will,

and Lowell in saying:

> Though the cause of Evil prosper,
> Yet 'tis Truth alone is strong,

and Tennyson in saying:

> I can but trust the good shall fall,
> At last—far off—at last, to all,
> And every winter change to spring.

II

The truth of this text is revealed in the contemporary struggle
between good in the form of freedom and justice, and evil
in the form of oppression and colonialism. Of the approximately 3,000,000,000 people in our world, more than
1,900,000,000—a vast majority—live on the continents of
Asia and Africa. Less than two decades ago most of the
Asian and African peoples were colonial subjects, dominated
politically, exploited economically, and segregated and humili-
ated by foreign powers. For years they protested against
these grave injustices. In nearly every territory in Asia and
Africa a courageous Moses pleaded passionately for the
freedom of his people. For more than twenty years Mahatma
Gandhi unrelentingly urged British viceroys, governors
general, prime ministers, and kings to let his people go. Like
the pharaohs of old, the British leaders turned deaf ears to
these agonizing pleas. Even the great Winston Churchill
responded to Gandhi's cry for independence by saying, "I
have not become the King's First Minister in order to preside
over the liquidation of the British Empire." The conflict
between two determined forces, the colonial powers and the
Asian and African peoples, has been one of the most momentous and critical struggles of the twentieth century.

But in spite of the resistance and recalcitrance of the
colonial powers, the victory of the forces of justice and

human dignity is gradually being achieved. Twenty-five years ago there were only three independent countries in the whole continent of Africa, but today thirty-two countries are independent. A short fifteen years ago the British Empire politically dominated more than 650,000,000 people in Asia and Africa, but today the number is less than 60,000,000. The Red Sea has opened. The oppressed masses in Asia and Africa have won their freedom from the Egypt of colonialism and now move toward the promised land of economic and cultural stability. These peoples see the evils of colonialism and imperialism dead upon the seashore.

In our own American struggle for freedom and justice, we are seeing the death of evil. In 1619, the Negro was brought to America from the soils of Africa. For more than two hundred years Africa was raped and plundered, her native kingdoms disorganized, and her people and rulers demoralized. In America, the Negro slave was merely a depersonalized cog in a vast plantation machine.

But there were those who had a nagging conscience and knew that so unjust a system represented a strange paradox in a nation founded on the principle that all men are created equal. In 1820, six years before his death, Thomas Jefferson wrote these melancholy words:

But the momentous question [slavery], like a fire-bell in the night, awakened and filled me with terror. I considered it at once as the knell of the Union. . . . I regret that I am now to die in the belief, that the useless sacrifice of themselves by the generation of 1776, to acquire self-government and happiness to their country, is to be thrown away . . . and my only consolation is to be, that I live not to weep over it.

Numerous abolitionists, like Jefferson, were tortured in their hearts by the question of slavery. With keen perception they saw that the immorality of slavery degraded the white master as well as the Negro.

Then came the day when Abraham Lincoln faced squarely this matter of slavery. His torments and vacillations are well known, yet the conclusion of his search is embodied in these words: "In giving freedom to the slave, we assure freedom to the free,—honourable alike in what we give and what we preserve." On this moral foundation Lincoln drafted the Emancipation Proclamation, an executive order that brought an end to chattel slavery. The significance of the Emancipation Proclamation was colourfully described by a great American, Frederick Douglass, in these words:

It recognizes and declares the real nature of the contest and places the North on the side of justice and civilization. . . . Unquestionably the first of January, 1863, is to be the most memorable in American annals. The Fourth of July was great, but the First of January, when we consider it in all its relations and bearings, is incomparably greater. The one had respect to the mere political birth of a nation; the last concerns the national life and character and is to determine whether that life and character shall be radiantly glorious with all high and noble virtues, or infamously blackened forevermore.

The Emancipation Proclamation did not, however, bring full freedom to the Negro, for although he enjoyed certain political and social opportunities during the Reconstruction, the Negro soon discovered that the pharaohs of the South were determined to keep him in slavery. Certainly the Emancipation Proclamation brought him nearer to the Red Sea, but it did not guarantee his passage through parted waters. Racial segregation, backed by a decision of the United States Supreme Court in 1896, was a new form of slavery disguised by certain niceties of complexity. In the great struggle of the last half century between the forces of justice attempting to end the evil system of segregation and the forces of injustice attempting to maintain it, the pharaohs have employed legal manœuvres, economic reprisals, and even physical violence to hold the Negro in the Egypt of segregation. Despite the patient cry of many a Moses, they refused to let the Negro people go.

Today we are witnessing a massive change. A world-shaking decree by the nine justices of the United States Supreme Court opened the Red Sea and the forces of justice are moving to the other side. The Court decreed an end to the old Plessy decision of 1896 and affirmed that separate facilities are inherently unequal and that to segregate a child on the basis of race is to deny the child an equal legal protection. This decision is a great beacon light of hope to millions of disinherited people. Looking back, we see the forces of segregation gradually dying on the seashore. The problem is far from solved and gigantic mountains of opposition lie ahead, but at least we have left Egypt, and with patient yet firm determination we shall reach the promised land. Evil in the form of injustice and exploitation shall not survive forever. A Red Sea passage in history ultimately brings the forces of goodness to victory, and the closing of the same waters marks the doom and destruction of the forces of evil.

All of this reminds us that evil carries the seed of its own destruction. In the long run right defeated is stronger than evil triumphant. Historian Charles A. Beard, when asked what major lessons he had learned from history, answered:

First, whom the gods would destroy they must first make mad with power. Second, the mills of God grind slowly, yet they grind exceeding small. Third, the bee fertilizes the flower it robs. Fourth, when it is dark enough you can see the stars.

These are the words, not of a preacher, but of a hardheaded historian, whose long and painstaking study of history revealed to him that evil has a self-defeating quality. It can go a long way, but then it reaches its limit. There is something in this universe that Greek mythology referred to as the goddess of Nemesis.

III

We must be careful at this point not to engage in a superficial optimism or to conclude that the death of a particular evil means that all evil lies dead upon the seashore. All progress is precarious, and the solution of one problem brings us face to face with another problem. The Kingdom of God as a universal reality is *not yet*. Because sin exists on every level of man's existence, the death of one tyranny is followed by the emergence of another tyranny.

But just as we must avoid a superficial optimism, we must also avoid a crippling pessimism. Even though all progress is precarious, within limits real social progress may be made. Although man's moral pilgrimage may never reach a destination point on earth, his never-ceasing strivings may bring him ever closer to the city of righteousness. And though the Kingdom of God may remain *not yet* as a universal reality in history, in the present it may exist in such isolated forms as in judgment, in personal devotion, and in some group life. "The kingdom of God is in the midst of you."

Above all, we must be reminded anew that God is at work in his universe. He is not outside the world looking on with a sort of cold indifference. Here on all the roads of life, he is striving in our striving. Like an ever-loving Father, he is working through history for the salvation of his children. As we struggle to defeat the forces of evil, the God of the universe struggles with us. Evil dies on the seashore, not merely because of man's endless struggle against it, but because of God's power to defeat it.

But why is God so slow in conquering the forces of evil? Why did God permit Hitler to kill six million Jews? Why did God permit slavery to continue in America for two hundred and forty-four years? Why does God permit blood-thirsty mobs to lynch Negro men and women at will and drown Negro boys and girls at whim? Why does not God break in and smash the evil schemes of wicked men?

I do not pretend to understand all of the ways of God or his particular timetable for grappling with evil. Perhaps if God dealt with evil in the overbearing way that we wish, he would defeat his ultimate purpose. We are responsible human beings, not blind automatons; persons, not puppets. By endowing us with freedom, God relinquished a measure of his own sovereignty and imposed certain limitations upon himself. If his children are free, they must do his will by a voluntary choice. Therefore, God cannot at the same time impose his will upon his children and also maintain his purpose for man. If through sheer omnipotence God were to defeat his purpose, he would express weakness rather than power. Power is the ability to fulfil purpose; action which defeats purpose is weakness.

God's unwillingness to deal with evil with an overbearing immediacy does not mean that he is doing nothing. We weak and finite human beings are not alone in our quest for the triumph of righteousness. There is, as Matthew Arnold wrote, an "enduring power, not ourselves, which makes for righteousness."

We must also remember that God does not forget his children who are the victims of evil forces. He gives us the interior resources to bear the burdens and tribulations of life. When we are in the darkness of some oppressive Egypt, God is a light unto our path. He imbues us with the strength needed to endure the ordeals of Egypt, and he gives us the courage and power to undertake the journey ahead. When the lamp of hope flickers and the candle of faith runs low, he restoreth our souls, giving us renewed vigour to carry on. He is with us not only in the noontime of fulfilment, but also in the midnight of despair.

In India Mrs. King and I spent a lovely weekend in the State of Karala, the southernmost point of that vast country. While there we visited the beautiful beach on Cape Comorin, which is called "Land's End," because this is actually where the land of India comes to an end. Nothing stretches before you except the broad expanse of rolling waters. This beautiful spot is a point at which meet three great bodies of water, the Indian Ocean, the Arabian Sea, and the Bay of Bengal. Seated on a huge rock that slightly protrudes into the ocean, we were enthralled by the vastness of the ocean and its terrifying immensities. As the waves unfolded in almost rhythmic succession and crashed against the base of the rock on which we were seated, an oceanic music brought sweetness to the ear. To the west we saw the magnificent sun, a great cosmic ball of fire, appear to sink into the very ocean itself. Just as it was almost lost from sight, Mrs. King touched me and said, "Look, Martin, isn't that beautiful!" I looked around and saw the moon, another ball of scintillating beauty. As the sun appeared to be sinking into the ocean, the moon appeared to be rising from the ocean.

When the sun finally passed completely beyond sight, darkness engulfed the earth, but in the east the radiant light of the rising moon shone supreme.

To my wife I said, "This is an analogy of what often happens in life." We have experiences when the light of day vanishes, leaving us in some dark and desolate midnight—moments when our highest hopes are turned into shambles of despair or when we are the victims of some tragic injustice and some terrible exploitation. During such moments our spirits are almost overcome by gloom and despair, and we feel that there is no light anywhere. But ever and again, we look toward the east and discover that there is another light which shines even in the darkness, and "the spear of frustration" is transformed "into a shaft of light."

This would be an unbearable world were God to have only a single light, but we may be consoled that God has two lights: a light to guide us in the brightness of the day when hopes are fulfilled and circumstances are favourable, and a light to guide us in the darkness of the midnight when we are thwarted and the slumbering giants of gloom and hopelessness rise in our souls. The testimony of the Psalmist is that we need never walk in darkness:

> Whither shall I go from thy spirit? or whither shall I flee from thy presence? If I ascend up into heaven, thou art there: if I make my bed in hell, behold, thou art there. If I take the wings of the morning, and dwell in the uttermost parts of the sea; even there shall thy hand lead me, and thy right hand shall hold me. If I say, Surely the darkness shall cover me; even the night shall be light about me. Yea, the darkness hideth not from thee; but the night shineth as the day: the darkness and the light are both alike to thee.

This faith will sustain us in our struggle to escape from the bondage of every evil Egypt. This faith will be a lamp unto our weary feet and a light unto our meandering path. Without such faith, man's highest dreams will pass silently to the dust.

CHAPTER NINE

Shattered dreams

*Whensoever I take my journey into
Spain, I will come to you.*
                              Romans 15:24

One of the most agonizing problems within our human
experience is that few, if any, of us live to see our fondest
hopes fulfilled. The hopes of our childhood and the promises
of our mature years are unfinished symphonies. In a famous
painting, George Frederic Watts portrays Hope as a tranquil
figure who, seated atop our planet, her head sadly bowed,
plucks a single unbroken harpstring. Is there any one of
us who has not faced the agony of blasted hopes and
shattered dreams?

In Paul's letter to the Roman Christians we find a potent
illustration of this vexing problem of disappointed hopes:
"Whensoever I take my journey into Spain, I will come to
you." One of his ardent hopes was to travel to Spain where,
at the edge of the then known world, he might further
proclaim the Christian gospel. On his return he wished to
have personal fellowship with that valiant group of Roman
Christians. The more he anticipated this privilege, the more
his heart quickened with joy. His preparations now centred
in carrying the gospel to the capital city of Rome and to
Spain at the distant fringe of the empire.

What a glowing hope stirred within Paul's heart! But he
never got to Rome according to the pattern of his hopes.
Because of his daring faith in Jesus Christ, he was indeed
taken there but as a prisoner and was held captive in a

little prison cell. Nor did he ever walk the dusty roads of Spain, nor look upon its curvacious slopes, nor watch its busy coastal life. He was put to death, we presume, as a martyr for Christ in Rome. Paul's life is a tragic story of a shattered dream.

Life mirrors many similar experiences. Who has not set out toward some distant Spain, some momentous goal, or some glorious realization, only to learn at last that he must settle for much less? We never walk as free men through the streets of our Rome; instead, circumstances decree that we live within little confining cells. Written across our lives is a fatal flaw and within history runs an irrational and unpredictable vein. Like Abraham, we too sojourn in the land of promise, but so often we do not become "heirs with him of the same promise." Always our reach exceeds our grasp.

After struggling for years to achieve independence, Mahatma Gandhi witnessed a bloody religious war between the Hindus and the Moslems, and the subsequent division of India and Pakistan shattered his heart's desire for a united nation. Woodrow Wilson died before realizing the fulfilment of his consuming vision of a League of Nations. Many Negro slaves in America, having longed passionately for freedom, died before emancipation. After praying in the garden of Gethsemane that the cup might pass, Jesus, nonetheless, drank to the last bitter dregs. And the Apostle Paul repeatedly and fervently prayed that the "thorn" might be removed from his flesh, but the pain and annoyance continued to the end of his days. Shattered dreams are a hallmark of our mortal life.

I

Before we determine how to live in a world where our highest hopes are not satisfied, we must ask, What does one do under such circumstances?

One possible reaction is to distil all of our frustrations into a core of bitterness and resentment. The person who pursues this path is likely to develop a callous attitude, a cold heart, and a bitter hatred toward God, toward those with whom he lives, and toward himself. Because he cannot corner God or life, he releases his pent-up vindictiveness in hostility toward other people. He may be extremely cruel to his mate and inhuman to his children. In short, meanness becomes his dominating characteristic. He loves no one and requires love from no one. He trusts no one and does not expect others to trust him. He finds fault in everything and everybody, and he continually complains.

Such a reaction poisons the soul and scars the personality, always harming the person who harbours this feeling more than anyone else. Medical science reveals that such physical ailments as arthritis, gastric ulcer, and asthma have on occasion been encouraged by bitter resentments. Psychosomatic medicine, dealing with bodily sicknesses which come from mental illnesses, shows how deep resentment may result in physical deterioration.

Another common reaction by persons experiencing the blighting of hope is to withdraw completely into themselves and to become absolute introverts. No one is permitted to enter into their lives and they refuse to enter into the lives of others. Such persons give up the struggle of life, lose their zest for living, and attempt to escape by lifting their minds to a transcendent realm of cold indifference. Detachment is the word which best describes them. Too unconcerned to love and too passionless to hate, too detached to be selfish and too life-less to be unselfish, too indifferent to experience joy and too cold to experience sorrow, they are neither dead nor alive; they merely exist. Their eyes do not see the beauties of nature, their ears are insensitive to the majestic sounds of great music, and their hands are even unresponsive to the touch of a charming little baby. Nothing of the aliveness of life is left in them; only the dull motion of bare existence. Disappointed hopes lead them to a crippling cynicism such as Omar Khayyám described:

> The Worldly Hope men set their Hearts upon
> Turns Ashes—or it prospers; and anon,

> Like Snow upon the Desert's dusty Face,
> Lighting a little hour or two—is gone.

This reaction is based on an attempt to escape from life. Psychiatrists say that when individuals attempt to escape from reality their personalities become thinner and thinner until finally they split. This is one of the causal sources of the schizophrenic personality.

A third way by which persons respond to disappointments in life is to adopt a fatalistic philosophy stipulating that whatever happens must happen and that all events are determined by necessity. Fatalism implies that everything is foreordained and inescapable. People who subscribe to this philosophy succumb to an absolute resignation to that which they consider to be their fate and think of themselves as being little more than helpless orphans cast into the terrifying immensities of space. Because they believe that man has no freedom, they seek neither to deliberate nor to make decisions, but rather they wait passively for external forces to decide for them. They never actively seek to change their circumstances, for they believe that all circumstances, as in the Greek tragedies, are controlled by irresistible and foreordained forces. Some fatalists are very religious people who think of God as the determiner and controller of destiny. This view is expressed in a verse of one of our Christian hymns:

> Though dark my path and sad my lot,
> Let me be still and murmur not,
> But breathe the prayer divinely taught,
> Thy will be done.

Fatalists, believing that freedom is a myth, surrender to a paralyzing determinism which concludes that we are

> But helpless Pieces of the Game He plays
> Upon this Chequer-board of Nights and Days;

and that we need not trouble about the future, for

> The Moving Finger writes; and, having writ,
> Moves on: nor all your Piety nor Wit
> Shall lure it back to cancel half a Line,
> Nor all your Tears wash out a Word of it.

To sink in the quicksands of fatalism is both intellectually and psychologically stifling. Because freedom is a part of the essence of man, the fatalist, by denying freedom, becomes a puppet, not a person. He is, of course, right in his conviction that there is no absolute freedom and that freedom always operates within the context of predestined structure. Common experience teaches that a man is free to go north from Atlanta to Washington or south from Atlanta to Miami, but not north to Miami nor south to Washington. Freedom is always within the framework of destiny. *But there is freedom.* We are both free and destined. Freedom is the act of deliberating, deciding, and responding within our destined nature. Even though destiny may prevent our going to some attractive Spain, we do have the capacity to accept such a disappointment, to respond to it, and to do something about the disappointment itself. But fatalism stymies the individual, leaving him helplessly inadequate for life.

Fatalism, furthermore, is based on an appalling conception of God, for everything, whether good or evil, is considered to represent the will of God. A healthy religion rises above the idea that God wills evil. Although God permits evil in order to preserve the freedom of man, he does not cause evil. That which is willed is intended, and the thought that God intends for a child to be born blind or for a man to suffer the ravages of insanity is sheer heresy that pictures God as a devil rather than as a loving Father. The embracing of fatalism is as tragic and dangerous a way to meet the problem of unfulfilled dreams as are bitterness and withdrawal.

II

What, then, is the answer? The answer lies in our willing acceptance of unwanted and unfortunate circumstances even as we still cling to a radiant hope, our acceptance of finite disappointment even as we adhere to infinite hope. This is not the grim, bitter acceptance of the fatalist, but the achievement found in Jeremiah's words, "This is a grief, and I must bear it."

You must honestly confront your shattered dream. To follow the escapist method of attempting to put the disappointment out of your mind will lead to a psychologically injurious repression. Place your failure at the forefront of your mind and stare daringly at it. Ask yourself, "How may I transform this liability into an asset? How may I, confined in some narrow Roman cell and unable to reach life's Spain, transmute this dungeon of shame into a haven of redemptive suffering?" Almost anything that happens to us may be woven into the purposes of God. It may lengthen our cords of sympathy. It may break our self-centred pride. The cross, which was willed by wicked men, was woven by God into the tapestry of world redemption.

Many of the world's most influential personalities have exchanged their thorns for crowns. Charles Darwin, suffering from a recurrent physical illness; Robert Louis Stevenson, plagued with tuberculosis; and Helen Keller, inflicted with blindness and deafness, responded not with bitterness or fatalism, but rather by the exercise of a dynamic will transformed negative circumstances into positive assets. Writes the biographer of George Frederick Handel:

His health and his fortunes had reached the lowest ebb. His right side had become paralyzed, and his money was all gone. His creditors seized him and threatened him with imprisonment. For a brief time he was tempted to give up the fight—but then he rebounded again to compose the greatest of his inspirations, the epic *Messiah*.

The "Hallelujah Chorus" was born, not in a sequestered villa in Spain, but in a narrow, undesirable cell.

How familiar is the experience of longing for Spain and settling for a Roman prison, and how less familiar the transforming of the broken remains of a disappointed expectation into opportunities to serve God's purpose! Yet powerful living always involves such victories over one's own soul and one's situation.

We Negroes have long dreamed of freedom, but still we are confined in an oppressive prison of segregation and discrimination. Must we respond with bitterness and cynicism? Certainly not, for this will destroy and poison our persona-

lities. Must we, by concluding that segregation is within the
will of God, resign ourselves to oppression? Of course not,
for this blasphemously attributes to God that which is of the
devil. To co-operate passively with an unjust system makes
the oppressed as evil as the oppressor. Our most fruitful
course is to stand firm with courageous determination, move
forward nonviolently amid obstacles and setbacks, accept
disappointments, and cling to hope. Our determined refusal
not to be stopped will eventually open the door of fulfilment. While still in the prison of segregation, we must ask,
"How may we turn this liability into an asset?" By recognizing the necessity of suffering in a righteous cause, we
may possibly achieve our humanity's full stature. To guard
ourselves from bitterness, we need the vision to see in this
generation's ordeals the opportunity to transfigure both ourselves and American society. Our present suffering and our
nonviolent struggle to be free may well offer to Western
civilization the kind of spiritual dynamic so desperately
needed for survival.

Some of us, of course, will die without having received
the realization of freedom, but we must continue to sail on
our charted course. We must accept finite disappointment,
but we must never lose infinite hope. Only in this way shall
we live without the fatigue of bitterness and the drain of
resentment.

This was the secret of the survival of our slave foreparents.
Slavery was a low, dirty, and inhuman business. When the
slaves were taken from Africa, they were cut off from their
family ties and chained to ships like beasts. Nothing is more
tragic than to be divorced from family, language, and roots.
In many instances, husbands were separated from wives and
children from parents. When women were forced to satisfy
the biological urges of white masters, slave husbands were
powerless to intervene. Yet, in spite of inexpressible cruelties,
our foreparents survived. When a new morning offered only
the same long rows of cotton, sweltering heat, and the rawhide whip of the overseer these brave and courageous men
and women dreamed of the brighter day. They had no
alternative except to accept the fact of slavery, but they

clung tenaciously to the hope of freedom. In a seemingly hopeless situation, they fashioned within their souls a creative optimism that strengthened them. Their bottomless vitality transformed the darkness of frustration into the light of hope.

III

I first flew from New York to London in the propeller-type aircraft that required nine and a half hours for a flight now made in six hours by jet. When returning from London to the States, I was told that the flying time would be twelve and a half hours. The distance was the same. Why an additional three hours? When the pilot entered the cabin to greet the passengers, I asked him to explain the difference in flight time. "You must understand something about the winds," he said. "When we leave New York, a strong tail wind is in our favour, but when we return, a strong head wind is against us." Then he added, "Don't worry. These four engines are capable of battling the winds." At times in our lives the tail winds of joy, triumph, and fulfilment favour us, and at times the head winds of disappointment, sorrow, and tragedy beat unrelentingly against us. Shall we permit adverse winds to overwhelm us as we journey across life's mighty Atlantic, or will our inner spiritual engines sustain us in spite of the winds? Our refusal to be stopped, our "courage to be," our determination to go on "in spite of," reveal the divine image within us. The man who has made this discovery knows that no burden can overwhelm him and no wind of adversity can blow his hope away. He can stand anything that can happen to him.

Certainly the Apostle Paul possessed this type of "courage to be." His life was a continual round of disappointments. On every side were broken plans and shattered dreams. Planning to visit Spain, he was consigned to a Roman prison. Hoping to go to Bithynia, he was sidetracked to Troas. His gallant mission for Christ was measured "in journeyings often, in perils of waters, in perils of robbers, in perils of mine own countrymen, in perils by the heathen, in perils in the city, in perils in the wilderness, in perils in the sea, in perils among false brethren." Did he permit these conditions to master him? "I have learned," he testified, "in whatsoever state I am, therewith to be content." Not that Paul had learned to be complacent, for nothing in his life characterizes him as a complacent individual. In his *Decline and Fall of the Roman Empire*, Edward Gibbon records, "Paul has done more to promote the idea of freedom and liberty than any man who set foot on western soil." Does this sound like complacency? Nor did he learn resignation to inscrutable fate. By discovering the distinction between spiritual tranquillity and the outward accidents of circumstance, Paul learned to stand tall and without despairing amid the disappointments of life.

Each of us who makes this magnificent discovery will, like Paul, be a recipient of that true peace "which passeth all understanding." Peace as the world commonly understands it comes when the summer sky is clear and the sun shines in scintillating beauty, when the pocketbook is full, when the mind and body are free of ache and pain, and when the shores of Spain have been reached. But this is not true peace. The peace of which Paul spoke is a calmness of soul amid terrors of trouble, inner tranquillity amid the howl and rage of outer storm, the serene quiet at the centre of a hurricane amid the howling and jostling winds. We readily understand the meaning of peace when everything is going right and when one is "up and in," but we are baffled when Paul speaks of that true peace which comes when a man is "down and out," when burdens lie heavy upon his shoulders, when pain throbs annoyingly in his body, when he is confined by the stone walls of a prison cell, and when disappointment is inescapably real. True peace, a calm that exceeds all description and all explanation, is peace amid storm and tranquillity amid disaster.

Through faith we may inherit Jesus' legacy, "Peace I leave with you, my peace I give unto you." Paul at Philippi, incarcerated in a dark and desolate dungeon, his body beaten and bloody, his feet chained, and his spirit tired, joyously sang the songs of Zion at midnight. The early Christians, facing hungry lions in the arena and the excruciating pain of the chopping block, rejoiced that they had been deemed worthy to suffer for the sake of Christ. Negro slaves, bone-weary in the sizzling heat and the marks of whip lashes freshly etched on their backs, sang triumphantly, "By and by I'm gwin to lay down this heavy load." These are living examples of peace that passeth all understanding.

Our capacity to deal creatively with shattered dreams is ultimately determined by our faith in God. Genuine faith imbues us with the conviction that beyond time is a divine Spirit and beyond life is Life. However dismal and catastrophic may be the present circumstances, we know we are not alone, for God dwells with us in life's most confining and oppressive cells. And even if we die there without having received the earthly promise, he shall lead us down that mysterious road called death and at last to that indescribable city he has prepared for us. His creative power is not exhausted by this earthly life, nor is his majestic love locked within the limited walls of time and space. Would not this be a strangely irrational universe if God did not ultimately join virtue and fulfilment, and an absurdly meaningless universe if death were a blind alley leading the human race into a state of nothingness? God through Christ has taken the sting from death by freeing us from its dominion. Our earthly life is a prelude to a glorious new awakening, and death is an open door that leads us into life eternal.

The Christian faith makes it possible for us nobly to accept that which cannot be changed, to meet disappointments and sorrow with an inner poise, and to absorb the most intense pain without abandoning our sense of hope, for we know, as Paul testified, in life or in death, in Spain or in Rome, "that all things work together for good to them that love God, to them who are the called according to his purpose."

CHAPTER TEN

How should a Christian view Communism

*Let judgment roll down as waters, and
righteousness as a mighty stream.*
                                        Amos 5:24

Few issues demand a more thorough and sober discussion than that presented by Communism. For at least three reasons every Christian minister should feel obligated to speak to his people on this controversial theme.

The first reason recognizes that the widespread influence of Communism has, like a mighty tidal wave, spread through Russia, China, Eastern Europe, and now even to our hemisphere. Nearly a thousand million of the peoples of the world believe in its teachings, many of them embracing it as a new religion to which they have surrendered completely. Such a force cannot be ignored.

A second reason is that Communism is the only serious rival to Christianity. Such great world religions as Judaism, Buddhism, Hinduism, and Mohammedanism are possible alternatives to Christianity, but no one conversant with the hard facts of the modern world will deny that Communism is Christianity's most formidable rival.

A third reason is that it is unfair and certainly unscientific to condemn a system before we know what that system teaches and why it is wrong.

Let me state clearly the basic premise of this sermon: Communism and Christianity are fundamentally incompatible. A true Christian cannot be a true Communist, for the

two philosophies are antithetical and all the dialectics of the
logicians cannot reconcile them. Why is this true?

I

First, Communism is based on a materialistic and humanistic
view of life and history. According to Communist theory,
matter, not mind or spirit, speaks the last word in the universe.
Such a philosophy is avowedly secularistic and atheistic.
Under it, God is merely a figment of the imagination, religion is a product of fear and ignorance, and the church is
an invention of the rulers to control the masses. Moreover,
Communism, like humanism, thrives on the grand illusion
that man, unaided by any divine power, can save himself and
usher in a new society—

> I fight alone, and win or sink,
> I need no one to make me free;
> I want no Jesus Christ to think,
> That He could ever die for me.

Cold atheism wrapped in the garments of materialism, Communism provides no place for God or Christ.

At the centre of the Christian faith is the affirmation that
there is a God in the universe who is the ground and essence
of all reality. A Being of infinite love and boundless power,
God is the creator, sustainer, and conserver of values. In
opposition to Communism's atheistic materialism, Christianity posits a theistic idealism. Reality cannot be explained
by matter in motion or the push and pull of economic forces.
Christianity affirms that at the heart of reality is a Heart, a
loving Father who works through history for the salvation
of his children. Man cannot save himself, for man is not
the measure of all things and humanity is not God. Bound
by the chains of his own sin and finiteness, man needs a
Saviour.

Second, Communism is based on ethical relativism and
accepts no stable moral absolutes. Right and wrong are relative to the most expedient methods for dealing with class
war. Communism exploits the dreadful philosophy that the

end justifies the means. It enunciates movingly the theory of a classless society, but alas! its methods for achieving this noble end are all too often ignoble. Lying, violence, murder, and torture are considered to be justifiable means to achieve the millennial end. Is this an unfair indictment? Listen to the words of Lenin, the real tactician of Communist theory: "We must be ready to employ trickery, deceit, lawbreaking, withholding and concealing truth." Modern history has known many tortuous nights and horror-filled days because his followers have taken this statement seriously.

In contrast to the ethical relativism of Communism, Christianity sets forth a system of absolute moral values and affirms that God has placed within the very structure of this universe certain moral principles that are fixed and immutable. The law of love as an imperative is the norm for all of man's actions. Furthermore, Christianity at its best refuses to live by a philosophy of ends justifying means. Destructive means cannot bring constructive ends, because the means represent the-ideal-in-the-making and the-end-in-progress. Immoral means cannot bring moral ends, for the ends are pre-existent in the means.

Third, Communism attributes ultimate value to the state. Man is made for the state and not the state for man. One may object, saying that in Communist theory the state is an "interim reality," which will "wither away" when the classless society emerges. True—in theory; but it is also true that, while it lasts, the state is the end. Man is a means to that end. Man has no inalienable rights. His only rights are derived from, and conferred by, the state. Under such a system, the fountain of freedom runs dry. Restricted are man's liberties of press and assembly, his freedom to vote, and his freedom to listen and to read. Art, religion, education, music, and science come under the gripping yoke of governmental control. Man must be a dutiful servant to the omnipotent state.

All of this is contrary, not only to the Christian doctrine of God, but also to the Christian estimate of man. Christianity insists that man is an end because he is a child of God, made in God's image. Man is more than a producing animal guided by economic forces; he is a being of spirit, crowned with glory and honour, endowed with the gift of freedom. The ultimate weakness of Communism is that it robs man of that quality which makes him man. Man, says Paul Tillich, is man because he is free. This freedom is expressed through man's capacity to deliberate, decide, and respond. Under Communism, the individual soul is shackled by the chains of conformity; his spirit is bound by the manacles of party allegiance. He is stripped of both conscience and reason. The trouble with Communism is that it has neither a theology nor a Christology; therefore it emerges with a mixed-up anthropology. Confused about God, it is also confused about man. In spite of its glowing talk about the welfare of the masses, Communism's methods and philosophy strip man of his dignity and worth, leaving him as little more than a depersonalized cog in the ever-turning wheel of the state.

Clearly, then, all of this is out of harmony with the Christian view of things. We must not fool ourselves. These systems of thought are too contradictory to be reconciled; they represent diametrically opposed ways of looking at the world and of transforming it. We should as Christians pray for the Communist constantly, but never can we, as true Christians, tolerate the philosophy of Communism.

Yet, something in the spirit and threat of Communism challenges us. The late Archbishop of Canterbury, William Temple, referred to Communism as a Christian heresy. He meant that Communism had laid hold on certain truths which are essential parts of the Christian view of things, although bound to them are theories and practices which no Christian could ever accept.

II

The theory, though surely not the practice, of Communism challenges us to be more concerned about social justice. With all of its false assumptions and evil methods, Communism arose as a protest against the injustices and indignities inflicted upon the underprivileged. *The Communist*

Manifesto was written by men aflame with a passion for social justice. Karl Marx, born of Jewish parents who both came from rabbinic stock, and trained, as he must have been, in the Hebrew Scriptures, could never forget the words of Amos: "Let judgment roll down as waters, and righteousness as a mighty stream." Marx's parents adopted Christianity when he was a child of six, thus adding to the Old Testament heritage that of the New. In spite of his later atheism and anti-ecclesiasticism, Marx could not quite forget Jesus' concern for "the least of these." In his writings, he champions the cause of the poor, the exploited, and the disinherited.

Communism in theory emphasizes a classless society. Although the world knows from sad experience that Communism has created new classes and a new lexicon of injustice, in its theoretical formulation it envisages a world society transcending the superficialities of race and colour, class and caste. Membership in the Communist party theoretically is not determined by the colour of a man's skin or the quality of blood in his veins.

Christians are bound to recognize any passionate concern for social justice. Such concern is basic in the Christian doctrine of the Fatherhood of God and the brotherhood of man. The Gospels abound with expressions of concern for the welfare of the poor. Listen to the words of the Magnificat: "He hath put down the mighty from their seats, and exalted them of low degree. He hath filled the hungry with good things; and the rich he hath sent empty away." No doctrinaire Communist ever expressed a passion for the poor and oppressed such as we find in the Manifesto of Jesus which affirms: "The Spirit of the Lord is upon me, because he hath anointed me to preach the gospel to the poor; he hath sent me to heal the brokenhearted, to preach deliverance to the captives, and recovering of sight to the blind, to set at liberty them that are bruised, to preach the acceptable year of the Lord."

Christians are also bound to recognize the ideal of a world unity in which all barriers of caste and colour are abolished. Christianity repudiates racism. The broad universalism standing at the centre of the gospel makes both the theory and practice of racial injustice morally unjustifiable. Racial prejudice is a blatant denial of the unity which we have in Christ, for in Christ there is neither Jew nor Gentile, bond nor free, Negro nor white.

In spite of the noble affirmations of Christianity, the church has often lagged in its concern for social justice and too often has been content to mouth pious irrelevances and sanctimonious trivialities. It has often been so absorbed in a future good "over yonder" that it forgets the present evils "down here." Yet the church is challenged to make the gospel of Jesus Christ relevant within the social situation. We must come to see that the Christian gospel is a two-way road. On the one side, it seeks to change the souls of men and thereby unite them with God; on the other, it seeks to change the environmental conditions of men so that the soul will have a chance after it is changed. Any religion that professes to be concerned with the souls of men and yet is not concerned with the economic and social conditions that strangle them and the social conditions that cripple them is the kind the Marxist describes as "an opiate of the people."

Honesty also impels us to admit that the church has not been true to its social mission on the question of racial justice. In this area it has failed Christ miserably. This failure is due, not only to the fact that the church has been appallingly silent and disastrously indifferent to the realm of race relations, but even more to the fact that it has often been an active participant in shaping and crystallizing the patterns of the race-caste system. Colonialism could not have been perpetuated if the Christian Church had really taken a stand against it. One of the chief defenders of the vicious system of apartheid in South Africa today is the Dutch Reformed Protestant Church. In America slavery could not have existed for almost two hundred and fifty years if the church had not sanctioned it, nor could segregation and discrimination exist today if the Christian Church were not a silent and often vocal partner. We must face the shameful fact that the church is the most segregated major institution in American society, and the most segregated hour of the week is, as Professor

Liston Pope has pointed out, eleven o'clock on Sunday morning. How often the church has been an echo rather than a voice, a tail-light behind the Supreme Court and other secular agencies, rather than a headlight guiding men progressively and decisively to higher levels of understanding.

The judgment of God is upon the church. The church has a schism in its own soul that it must close. It will be one of the tragedies of Christian history if future historians record that at the height of the twentieth century the church was one of the greatest bulwarks of white supremacy.

III

In the face of the Communist challenge we must examine honestly the weaknesses of traditional capitalism. In all fairness, we must admit that capitalism has often left a gulf between superfluous wealth and abject poverty, has created conditions permitting necessities to be taken from the many to give luxuries to the few, and has encouraged small-hearted men to become cold and conscienceless so that, like Dives before Lazarus, they are unmoved by suffering, poverty-stricken humanity. Although through social reform American capitalism is doing much to reduce such tendencies, there is much yet to be accomplished. God intends that all of his children shall have the basic necessities for meaningful, healthful life. Surely it is unchristian and unethical for some to wallow in the soft beds of luxury while others sink in the quicksands of poverty.

The profit motive, when it is the sole basis of an economic system, encourages a cut-throat competition and selfish ambition that inspires men to be more concerned about making a living than making a life. It can make men so I-centred that they no longer are Thou-centred. Are we not too prone to judge success by the index of our salaries and the size of the wheel base on our automobiles, and not by the quality of our service and relationship to humanity? Capitalism may lead to a practical materialism that is as pernicious as the theoretical materialism taught by Communism.

We must honestly recognize that truth is not to be found either in traditional capitalism or in Marxism. Each represents a partial truth. Historically, capitalism failed to discern the truth in collective enterprise and Marxism failed to see the truth in individual enterprise. Nineteenth-century capitalism failed to appreciate that life is social and Marxism failed, and still fails, to see that life is individual and social. The Kingdom of God is neither the thesis of individual enterprise nor the antithesis of collective enterprise, but a synthesis which reconciles the truth of both.

IV

Finally, we are challenged to dedicate our lives to the cause of Christ even as the Communists dedicate theirs to Communism. We who cannot accept the creed of the Communists recognize their zeal and commitment to a cause which they believe will create a better world. They have a sense of purpose and destiny, and they work passionately and assiduously to win others to Communism. How many Christians are as concerned to win others to Christ? Often we have neither zeal for Christ nor zest for his kingdom. For so many Christians, Christianity is a Sunday activity having no relevancy for Monday and the church is little more than a secular social club having a thin veneer of religiosity. Jesus is an ancient symbol whom we do the honour of calling Christ, and yet his Lordship is neither affirmed nor acknowledged by our substanceless lives. Would that the Christian fire were burning in the hearts of all Christians with the same intensity as the Communist fire is burning in the hearts of Communists! Is Communism alive in the world today because we have not been Christian enough?

We need to pledge ourselves anew to the cause of Christ. We must recapture the spirit of the early church. Wherever the early Christians went, they made a triumphant witness for Christ. Whether on the village streets or in the city jails, they daringly proclaimed the good news of the gospel. Their reward for this audacious witness was often the excruciating agony of a lion's den or the poignant pain of a chopping block, but they continued in the faith that they had discovered a cause so great and had been transformed by a Saviour so divine that even death was not too great a sacrifice. When they entered a town, the power structure became disturbed. Their new gospel brought the refreshing warmth of spring to men whose lives had been hardened by the long winter of traditionalism. They urged men to revolt against old systems of injustice and old structures of immorality. When the rulers objected, these strange people, intoxicated with the wine of God's grace, continued to proclaim the gospel until even men and women in Caesar's household were convinced, until jailers dropped their keys, and until kings trembled on their thrones. T. R. Glover has written that the early Christians "out-thought, out-lived, and out-died" everyone else.

Where is that kind of fervour today? Where is that kind of daring, revolutionary commitment to Christ today? Is it hidden behind smoke screens and altars? Is it buried in a grave called respectability? Is it inextricably bound with nameless status quos and imprisoned within cells of stagnant mores? This devotion must again be released. Christ must once more be enthroned in our lives.

This is our best defence against Communism. War is not the answer. Communism will never be defeated by the use of atomic bombs or nuclear weapons. Let us not join those who shout war and who through their misguided passions urge the United States to relinquish its participation in the United Nations. These are days when Christians must evince wise restraint and calm reasonableness. We must not call everyone a Communist or an appeaser who recognizes that hate and hysteria are not the final answers to the problems of these turbulent days. We must not engage in a negative anti-Communism, but rather in a positive thrust for democracy, realizing that our greatest defence against Communism is to take offensive action in behalf of justice and righteousness. After our condemnation of the philosophy of Communism has been eloquently expressed, we must with positive action seek to remove those conditions of poverty, insecurity, injustice, and racial discrimination which are the fertile soil in which the seed of Communism grows and develops. Communism thrives only when the doors of opportunity are closed and human aspirations are stifled. Like the early Christians, we must move into a sometimes hostile world armed with the revolutionary gospel of Jesus Christ. With this powerful gospel we shall boldly challenge the status quo and unjust mores and thereby speed the day when "every valley shall be exalted, and every mountain and hill shall be made low: and the crooked shall be made straight, and the rough places plain: and the glory of the Lord shall be revealed."

Our hard challenge and our sublime opportunity is to bear witness to the spirit of Christ in fashioning a truly Christian world. If we accept the challenge with devotion and valour, the bell of history will toll for Communism, and we shall make the world safe for democracy and secure for the people of Christ.

CHAPTER ELEVEN

Our God is able

*Now unto him that is able to keep you
from falling.*   Jude 24

At the centre of the Christian faith is the conviction that in the universe there is a God of power who is able to do exceedingly abundant things in nature and in history. This conviction is stressed over and over in the Old and the New Testaments. Theologically, this affirmation is expressed in the doctrine of the omnipotence of God. The God whom we worship is not a weak and incompetent God. He is able to beat back gigantic waves of opposition and to bring low prodigious mountains of evil. The ringing testimony of the Christian faith is that God is able.

There are those who seek to convince us that only man is able. Their attempt to substitute a man-centred universe for a God-centred universe is not new. It had its modern beginnings in the Renaissance and subsequently in the Age of Reason, when some men gradually came to feel that God was an unnecessary item on the agenda of life. In these periods and later in the industrial revolution in England, others questioned whether God was any longer relevant. The laboratory began to replace the church, and the scientist became a substitute for the prophet. Not a few joined Swinburne in singing a new anthem: "Glory to Man in the highest! for Man is the master of things."

The devotees of the new man-centred religion point to the spectacular advances of modern science as justification for their faith. Science and technology have enlarged man's body. The telescope and television have enlarged his eyes. The telephone, radio, and microphone have strengthened his voice and ears. The automobile and aeroplane have lengthened his legs. The wonder drugs have prolonged his life. Have not these amazing achievements assured us that man is able?

But alas! something has shaken the faith of those who have made the laboratory "the new cathedral of men's hopes." The instruments which yesterday were worshipped today contain cosmic death, threatening to plunge all of us into the abyss of annihilation. Man is not able to save himself or the world. Unless he is guided by God's spirit, his new-found scientific power will become a devastating Frankenstein monster that will bring to ashes his earthly life.

At times other forces cause us to question the ableness of God. The stark and colossal reality of evil in the world—what Keats calls "the giant agony of the world"; ruthless floods and tornadoes that wipe away people as though they were weeds in an open field; ills like insanity plaguing some individuals from birth and reducing their days to tragic cycles of meaninglessness; the madness of war and the barbarity of man's inhumanity to man—why, we ask, do these things occur if God is able to prevent them? This problem, namely, the problem of evil, has always plagued the mind of man. I would limit my response to an assertion that much of the evil which we experience is caused by man's folly and ignorance and also by the misuse of his freedom. Beyond this, I can say only that there is and always will be a penumbra of mystery surrounding God. What appears at the moment to be evil may have a purpose that our finite minds are incapable of comprehending. So in spite of the presence of evil and the doubts that lurk in our minds, we shall wish not to surrender the conviction that our God is able.

I

Let us notice, first, that God is able to sustain the vast scope of the physical universe. Here again, we are tempted to feel that man is the true master of the physical universe. Man-made jet planes compress into minutes distances that formerly required weeks of tortuous effort. Man-made space ships carry cosmonauts through outer space at fantastic speeds. Is not God being replaced in the mastery of the cosmic order?

But before we are consumed too greatly by our man-centred arrogance, let us take a broader look at the universe. Will we not soon discover that our man-made instruments seem barely to be moving in comparison to the movement of the God-created solar system? Think about the fact, for instance, that the earth is circling the sun so fast that the fastest jet would be left sixty-six thousand miles behind in the first hour of a space race. In the past seven minutes we have been hurtled more than eight thousand miles through space. Or consider the sun which scientists tell us is the centre of the solar system. Our earth revolves around this cosmic ball of fire once each year, travelling 584,000,000 miles at the rate of 66,700 miles per hour or 1,600,000 miles per day. By this time tomorrow we shall be 1,600,000 miles from where we are at this hundredth of a second. The sun, which seems to be remarkably near, is 93,000,000 miles from the earth. Six months from now we shall be on the other side of the sun—93,000,000 miles beyond it— and in a year from now we shall have been swung completely around it and back to where we are right now. So when we behold the illimitable expanse of space, in which we are compelled to measure stellar distance in light years and in which heavenly bodies travel at incredible speeds, we are forced to look beyond man and affirm anew that God is able.

II

Let us notice that God is able to subdue all the powers of evil. In affirming that God is able to conquer evil we admit the reality of evil. Christianity has never dismissed evil as illusory, or an error of the mortal mind. It reckons with evil as a force that has objective reality. But Christianity contends that evil contains the seed of its own destruction. History is the story of evil forces that advance with seemingly irresistible power only to be crushed by the battering rams of the forces of justice. There is a law in the moral world—a silent, invisible imperative, akin to the laws in the physical world—which reminds us that life will work only in a certain way. The Hitlers and the Mussolinis have their day, and for a period they may wield great power, spreading themselves like a green bay tree, but soon they are cut down like the grass and wither as the green herb.

In his graphic account of the Battle of Waterloo in *Les Misérables*, Victor Hugo wrote:

Was it possible that Napoleon should win this battle? We answer no. Why? Because of Wellington? Because of Blücher? No. Because of God. . . . Napoleon had been impeached before the Infinite, and his fall was decreed. He vexed God. Waterloo is not a battle; it is the change of front of the universe.

In a real sense, Waterloo symbolizes the doom of every Napoleon and is an eternal reminder to a generation drunk with military power that in the long run of history might does not make right and the power of the sword cannot conquer the power of the spirit.

An evil system, known as colonialism, swept across Africa and Asia. But then the quiet invisible law began to operate. Prime Minister Macmillan said, "The wind of change began to blow." The powerful colonial empires began to disintegrate like stacks of cards, and new, independent nations began to emerge like refreshing oases in deserts sweltering under the heat of injustice. In less than fifteen years independence has swept through Asia and Africa like an irresistible tidal wave, releasing more than 1,500,000 people from the crippling manacles of colonialism.

In our own nation another unjust and evil system, known as segregation, for nearly one hundred years inflicted the Negro with a sense of inferiority, deprived him of his personhood, and denied him his birthright of life, liberty, and the pursuit of happiness. Segregation has been the Negroes' burden and America's shame. But as on the world scale, so in our nation, the wind of change began to blow. One event has followed another to bring a gradual end to the system of segregation. Today we know with certainty that segregation is dead. The only question remaining is how costly will be the funeral.

These great changes are not mere political and sociological shifts. They represent the passing of systems that were born in injustice, nurtured in inequality, and reared in exploitation. They represent the inevitable decay of any system based on principles that are not in harmony with the moral laws of the universe. When in future generations men look back upon these turbulent, tension-packed days through which we are passing, they will see God working through history for the salvation of man. They will know that God was working through those men who had the vision to perceive that no nation could survive half slave and half free.

God is able to conquer the evils of history. His control is never usurped. If at times we despair because of the relatively slow progress being made in ending racial discrimination and if we become disappointed because of the undue cautiousness of the federal government, let us gain new heart in the fact that God is able. In our sometimes difficult and often lonesome walk up freedom's road, we do not walk alone. God walks with us. He has placed within the very structure of this universe certain absolute moral laws. We can neither defy nor break them. If we disobey them, they will break us. The forces of evil may temporarily conquer truth, but truth will ultimately conquer its conqueror. Our God is able. James Russell Lowell was right:

Truth forever on the scaffold, Wrong forever on the
                                                      throne,—
Yet that scaffold sways the future, and, behind the dim
                                                      unknown,
Standeth God within the shadow, keeping watch above
                                                      his own.

III

Let us notice, finally, that God is able to give us interior
resources to confront the trials and difficulties of life. Each
of us faces circumstances in life which compel us to carry
heavy burdens of sorrow. Adversity assails us with hurricane
force. Glowing sunrises are transformed into darkest nights.
Our highest hopes are blasted and our noblest dreams are
shattered.

Christianity has never overlooked these experiences. They
come inevitably. Like the rhythmic alternation in the natural
order, life has the glittering sunlight of its summers and the
piercing chill of its winters. Days of unutterable joy are
followed by days of overwhelming sorrow. Life brings
periods of flooding and periods of drought. When these dark
hours of life emerge, many cry out with Paul Laurence
Dunbar:

      A crust of bread and a corner to sleep in,
      A minute to smile and an hour to weep in,
      A pint of joy to a peck of trouble,
      And never a laugh but the moans come double;
          And that is life!

Admitting the weighty problems and staggering disappointments, Christianity affirms that God is able to give us
the power to meet them. He is able to give us the inner
equilibrium to stand tall amid the trials and burdens of life.
He is able to provide inner peace amid outer storms. This
inner stability of the man of faith is Christ's chief legacy
to his disciples. He offers neither material resources nor a
magical formula that exempts us from suffering and persecution, but he brings an imperishable gift: "Peace I leave

with you." This is that peace which passeth all understanding.

At times we may feel that we do not need God, but on the day when the storms of disappointment rage, the winds of disaster blow, and the tidal waves of grief beat against our lives, if we do not have a deep and patient faith our emotional lives will be ripped to shreds. There is so much frustration in the world because we have relied on gods rather than God. We have genuflected before the god of science only to find that it has given us the atomic bomb, producing fears and anxieties that science can never mitigate. We have worshipped the god of pleasure only to discover that thrills play out and sensations are short-lived. We have bowed before the god of money only to learn that there are such things as love and friendship that money cannot buy and that in a world of possible depressions, stock market crashes, and bad business investments, money is a rather uncertain deity. These transitory gods are not able to save us or bring happiness to the human heart.

Only God is able. It is faith in him that we must rediscover. With this faith we can transform bleak and desolate valleys into sunlit paths of joy and bring new light into the dark caverns of pessimism. Is someone here moving toward the twilight of life and fearful of that which we call death? Why be afraid? God is able. Is someone here on the brink of despair because of the death of a loved one, the breaking of a marriage, or the waywardness of a child? Why despair? God is able to give you the power to endure that which cannot be changed. Is someone here anxious because of bad health? Why be anxious? Come what may, God is able.

As I come to the conclusion of my message, I would wish you to permit a personal experience. The first twenty-four years of my life were years packed with fulfilment. I had no basic problems or burdens. Because of concerned and loving parents who provided for my every need, I sallied through high school, college, theological school, and graduate school without interruption. It was not until I became a part of the leadership of the Montgomery bus protest that I was actually confronted with the trials of life. Almost immediately after the protest had been undertaken, we began to receive threatening telephone calls and letters in our home. Sporadic in the beginning, they increased day after day. At first I took them in my stride, feeling that they were the work of a few hotheads who would become discouraged after they discovered that we would not fight back. But as the weeks passed, I realized that many of the threats were in earnest. I felt myself faltering and growing in fear.

After a particularly strenuous day, I settled in bed at a late hour. My wife had already fallen asleep and I was about to doze off when the telephone rang. An angry voice said, "Listen, nigger, we've taken all we want from you. Before next week you'll be sorry you ever came to Montgomery." I hung up, but I could not sleep. It seemed that all of my fears had come down on me at once. I had reached the saturation point.

I got out of bed and began to walk the floor. Finally, I went to the kitchen and heated a pot of coffee. I was ready to give up. I tried to think of a way to move out of the picture without appearing to be a coward. In this state of exhaustion, when my courage had almost gone, I determined to take my problem to God. My head in my hands, I bowed over the kitchen table and prayed aloud. The words I spoke to God that midnight are still vivid in my memory. "I am here taking a stand for what I believe is right. But now I am afraid. The people are looking to me for leadership, and if I stand before them without strength and courage, they too will falter. I am at the end of my powers. I have nothing left. I've come to the point where I can't face it alone."

At that moment I experienced the presence of the Divine as I had never before experienced him. It seemed as though I could hear the quiet assurance of an inner voice, saying, "Stand up for righteousness, stand up for truth. God will be at your side forever." Almost at once my fears began to pass from me. My uncertainty disappeared. I was ready to face anything. The outer situation remained the same, but God had given me inner calm.

Three nights later, our home was bombed. Strangely

enough, I accepted the word of the bombing calmly. My experience with God had given me a new strength and trust. I knew now that God is able to give us the interior resources to face the storms and problems of life.

Let this affirmation be our ringing cry. It will give us courage to face the uncertainties of the future. It will give our tired feet new strength as we continue our forward stride toward the city of freedom. When our days become dreary with low-hovering clouds and our nights become darker than a thousand midnights, let us remember that there is a great benign Power in the universe whose name is God, and he is able to make a way out of no way, and transform dark yesterdays into bright tomorrows. This is our hope for becoming better men. This is our mandate for seeking to make a better world.

CHAPTER TWELVE

Antidotes for fear

*There is no fear in love; but perfect
love casteth out fear: because fear hath
torment. He that feareth is not made
perfect in love.*   I John 4:18

In these days of catastrophic change and calamitous uncertainty, is there any man who does not experience the depression and bewilderment of crippling fear, which, like a nagging
hound of hell, pursues our every footstep?

Everywhere men and women are confronted by fears that
often appear in strange disguises and a variety of ward-
robes. Haunted by the possibility of bad health, we detect
in every meaningless symptom an evidence of disease.
Troubled by the fact that days and years pass so quickly,
we dose ourselves with drugs which promise eternal youth.
If we are physically vigorous, we become so concerned by
the prospect that our personalities may collapse that we
develop an inferiority complex and stumble through life
with a feeling of insecurity, a lack of self-confidence, and
a sense of impending failure. A fear of what life may bring
encourages some persons to wander aimlessly along the frit-
tering road of excessive drink and sexual promiscuity. Almost
without being aware of the change, many people have permitted fear to transform the sunrise of love and peace into a
sunset of inner depression.

When unchecked, fear spawns a whole brood of phobias—
fear of water, high places, closed rooms, darkness, loneliness,

among others—and such an accumulation culminates in phobiaphobia or the fear of fear itself.

Especially common in our highly competitive society are economic fears, from which, Karen Horney says, come most of the psychological problems of our age. Captains of industry are tormented by the possible failure of their business and the capriciousness of the stock market. Employees are plagued by the prospect of unemployment and the consequences of an ever-increasing automation.

And consider, too, the multiplication in our day of religious and ontological fears, which include the fear of death and racial annihilation. The advent of the atomic age, which should have ushered in an era of plenty and of prosperity, has lifted the fear of death to morbid proportions. The terrifying spectacle of nuclear warfare has put Hamlet's words, "To be or not to be," on millions of trembling lips. Witness our frenzied efforts to construct fallout shelters. As though even these offer sanctuary from an H-bomb attack! Witness the agonizing desperation of our petitions that our government increase the nuclear stockpile. But our fanatical quest to maintain "a balance of terror" only increases our fear and leaves nations on tiptoes lest some diplomatic *faux pas* ignite a frightful holocaust.

Realizing that fear drains a man's energy and depletes his resources, Emerson wrote, "He has not learned the lesson of life who does not every day surmount a fear."

But I do not mean to suggest that we should seek to eliminate fear altogether from human life. Were this humanly possible, it would be practically undesirable. Fear is the elemental alarm system of the human organism which warns of approaching dangers and without which man could not have survived in either the primitive or modern worlds. Fear, moreover, is a powerfully creative force. Every great invention and intellectual advance represents a desire to escape from some dreaded circumstance or condition. The fear of darkness led to the discovery of the secret of electricity. The fear of pain led to the marvellous advances of medical science. The fear of ignorance was one reason that man built great institutions of learning. The fear of war was one of the forces behind the birth of the United Nations. Angelo Patri has rightly said, "Education consists in being afraid at the right time." If man were to lose his capacity to fear, he would be deprived of his capacity to grow, invent, and create. So in a sense fear is normal, necessary, and creative.

But we must remember that abnormal fears are emotionally ruinous and psychologically destructive. To illustrate the difference between normal and abnormal fear, Sigmund Freud spoke of a person who was quite properly afraid of snakes in the heart of an African jungle and of another person who neurotically feared that snakes were under the carpet in his city apartment. Psychologists say that normal children are born with only two fears—the fear of falling and the fear of loud noises—and that all others are environmentally acquired. Most of these acquired fears are snakes under the carpet.

It is to such fears that we usually refer when we speak of getting rid of fear. But this is only a part of the story. Normal fear protects us; abnormal fear paralyzes us. Normal fear motivates us to improve our individual and collective welfare; abnormal fear constantly poisons and distorts our inner lives. Our problem is not to be rid of fear but rather to harness and master it. How may it be mastered?

I

First, we must unflinchingly face our fears and honestly ask ourselves why we are afraid. This confrontation will, to some measure, grant us power. We shall never be cured of fear by escapism or repression, for the more we attempt to ignore and repress our fears, the more we multiply our inner conflicts.

By looking squarely and honestly at our fears we learn that many of them are residues of some childhood need or apprehension. Here, for instance, is a person haunted by a fear of death or the thought of punishment in the afterlife, who discovers that he has unconsciously projected into the whole of reality the childhood experience of being punished by parents, locked in a room, and seemingly deserted. Or here is a man plagued by the fear of inferiority and social rejection, who discovers that rejection in childhood by a self-centred mother and a preoccupied father left him with a self-defeating sense of inadequacy and a repressed bitterness toward life.

By bringing our fears to the forefront of consciousness, we may find them to be more imaginary than real. Some of them will turn out to be snakes under the carpet.

And let us also remember that, more often than not, fear involves the misuse of the imagination. When we get our fears into the open, we may laugh at some of them, and this is good. One psychiatrist said, "Ridicule is the master cure for fear and anxiety."

II

Second, we can master fear through one of the supreme virtues known to man: courage. Plato considered courage to be an element of the soul which bridges the cleavage between reason and desire. Aristotle thought of courage as the affirmation of man's essential nature. Thomas Aquinas said that courage is the strength of mind capable of conquering whatever threatens the attainment of the highest good.

Courage, therefore, is the power of the mind to overcome fear. Unlike anxiety, fear has a definite object which may be faced, analyzed, attacked, and, if need be, endured. How often the object of our fear is fear itself: In his *Journal* Henry David Thoreau wrote, "Nothing is so much to be feared as fear." Centuries earlier, Epictetus wrote, "For it is not death or hardship that is a fearful thing, but the fear of hardship and death." Courage takes the fear produced by a definite object into itself and thereby conquers the fear involved. Paul Tillich has written, "Courage is self-affirmation 'in spite of' . . . that which tends to hinder the self from affirming itself." It is self-affirmation in spite of death and nonbeing, and he who is courageous takes the fear of death into his self-affirmation and acts upon it. This courageous self-affirmation, which is surely a remedy for fear, is not selfishness, for self-affirmation includes both a proper self-love and a properly propositioned love of others. Erich Fromm has shown in convincing terms that the right kind of self-love and the right kind of love of others are interdependent.

Courage, the determination not to be overwhelmed by any object, however frightful, enables us to stand up to any fear. Many of our fears are not mere snakes under the carpet. Trouble is a reality in this strange medley of life, dangers lurk within the circumference of every action, accidents do occur, bad health is an ever-threatening possibility, and death is a stark, grim, and inevitable fact of human experience. Evil and pain in this conundrum of life are close to each of us, and we do both ourselves and our neighbours a great disservice when we attempt to prove that there is nothing in this world of which we should be frightened. These forces that threaten to negate life must be challenged by courage, which is the power of life to affirm itself in spite of life's ambiguities. This requires the exercise of a creative will that enables us to hew out a stone of hope from a mountain of despair.

Courage and cowardice are antithetical. Courage is an inner resolution to go forward in spite of obstacles and frightening situations; cowardice is a submissive surrender to circumstance. Courage breeds creative self-affirmation; cowardice produces destructive self-abnegation. Courage faces fear and thereby masters it; cowardice represses fear and is thereby mastered by it. Courageous men never lose the zest for living even though their life situation is zestless; cowardly men, overwhelmed by the uncertainties of life, lose the will to live. We must constantly build dykes of courage to hold back the flood of fear.

III

Third, fear is mastered through love. The New Testament affirms, "There is no fear in love; but perfect love casteth out fear." The kind of love which led Christ to a cross and kept Paul unembittered amid the angry torrents of persecution is not soft, anæmic, and sentimental. Such love confronts evil without flinching and shows in our popular parlance an infinite capacity "to take it." Such love overcomes the world even from a rough-hewn cross against the skyline.

But does love have a relationship to our modern fear of war, economic displacement, and racial injustice? Hate is rooted in fear, and the only cure for fear-hate is love. Our deteriorating international situation is shot through with the lethal darts of fear. Russia fears America, and America fears Russia. Likewise China and India, and the Israelis and the Arabs. These fears include another nation's aggression, scientific and technological supremacy, and economic power, and our own loss of status and power. Is not fear one of the major causes of war? We say that war is a consequence of hate, but close scrutiny reveals this sequence: first fear, then hate, then war, and finally deeper hatred. Were a nightmarish nuclear war to engulf our world, the cause would be not so much that one nation hated another, but that both nations feared each other.

What method has the sophisticated ingenuity of modern man employed to deal with the fear of war? We have armed ourselves to the nth degree. The West and the East have engaged in a fever-pitched arms race. Expenditures for defence have risen to mountainous proportions, and weapons of destruction have been assigned priority over all other human endeavours. The nations have believed that greater armaments will cast out fear. But alas! they have produced greater fear. In these turbulent, panic-stricken days we are once more reminded of the judicious words of old, "Perfect love casteth out fear." Not arms, but love, understanding, and organized goodwill can cast out fear. Only disarmament, based on good faith, will make mutual trust a living reality.

Our own problem of racial injustice must be solved by the same formula. Racial segregation is buttressed by such irrational fears as loss of preferred economic privilege, altered social status, intermarriage, and adjustment to new situations. Through sleepless nights and haggard days numerous white people attempt to combat these corroding fears by diverse methods. By following the path of escape, some seek to ignore the question of race relations and to close their mind to the issues involved. Others placing their faith in such legal manœuvres as interposition and nullification, counsel massive resistance. Still others hope to drown their fear by engaging in acts of violence and meanness toward their Negro brethren. But how futile are all these remedies! Instead of eliminating fear, they instil deeper and more pathological fears that leave the victims inflicted with strange psychoses and peculiar cases of paranoia. Neither repression, massive resistance, nor aggressive violence will cast out the fear of integration; only love and goodwill can do that.

If our white brothers are to master fear, they must depend not only on their commitment to Christian love but also on the Christlike love which the Negro generates toward them. Only through our adherence to love and nonviolence will the fear in the white community be mitigated. A guilt-ridden white minority fears that if the Negro attains power, he will without restraint or pity act to revenge the accumulated injustices and brutality of the years. A parent, who has continually mistreated his son, suddenly realizes that he is now taller than the parent. Will the son use his new physical power to repay for all of the blows of the past?

Once a helpless child, the Negro has now grown politically, culturally, and economically. Many white men fear retaliation. The Negro must show them that they have nothing to fear, for the Negro forgives and is willing to forget the past. *The Negro must convince the white man that he seeks justice for both himself and the white man.* A mass movement exercising love and nonviolence and demonstrating power under discipline should convince the white community that were such a movement to attain strength its power would be used creatively and not vengefully.

What then is the cure of this morbid fear of integration? We know the cure. God help us to achieve it! Love casts out fear.

This truth is not without a bearing on our personal anxieties. We are afraid of the superiority of other people, of failure, and of the scorn or disapproval of those whose opinions we most value. Envy, jealousy, a lack of self-confidence, a feeling of insecurity, and a haunting sense of inferiority are all rooted in fear. We do not envy people and then fear them; first we fear them and subsequently we become jealous of them. Is there a cure for these annoying fears that pervert our personal lives? Yes, a deep and abiding commitment to the way of love. "Perfect love casteth out fear."

Hatred and bitterness can never cure the disease of fear; only love can do that. Hatred paralyzes life; love releases it. Hatred confuses life; love harmonizes it. Hatred darkens life; love illumines it.

IV

Fourth, fear is mastered through faith. A common source of fear is an awareness of deficient resources and of a consequent inadequacy for life. All too many people attempt to face the tensions of life with inadequate spiritual resources. When vacationing in Mexico, Mrs. King and I wished to go deep-sea fishing. For reasons of economy, we rented an old and poorly equipped boat. We gave this little thought until, ten miles from shore, the clouds lowered and howling winds blew. Then we became paralyzed with fear, for we knew our boat was deficient. Multitudes of people are in a similar situation. Heavy winds and weak boats explain their fear.

Many of our abnormal fears can be dealt with by the skills of psychiatry, a relatively new discipline pioneered by Sigmund Freud, which investigates the subconscious drives of men and seeks to discover how and why fundamental energies are diverted into neurotic channels. Psychiatry helps us to look candidly at our inner selves and to search out the causes of our failures and fears. But much of our fearful living encompasses a realm where the service of psychiatry is ineffectual unless the psychiatrist is a man of religious faith. For our trouble is simply that we attempt to confront fear without faith; we sail through the stormy seas of life without adequate spiritual boats. One of the leading physicians in America has said, "The only known cure for fear is faith."

Abnormal fears and phobias that are expressed in neurotic anxiety may be cured by psychiatry; but the fear of death, nonbeing, and nothingness, expressed in existential anxiety, may be cured only by a positive religious faith.

A positive religious faith does not offer an illusion that we shall be exempt from pain and suffering, nor does it imbue us with the idea that life is a drama of unalloyed comfort and untroubled ease. Rather, it instils us with the inner equilibrium needed to face strains, burdens, and fears that inevitably come, and assures us that the universe is trustworthy and that God is concerned.

Irreligion, on the other hand, would have us believe that we are orphans cast into the terrifying immensities of space in a universe that is without purpose or intelligence. Such a view drains courage and exhausts the energies of men. In his *Confession* Tolstoi wrote concerning the aloneness and emptiness he felt before his conversion:

There was a period in my life when everything seemed to be crumbling, the very foundations of my convictions were beginning to give way, and I felt myself going to pieces. There was no sustaining influence in my life and there was no God there, and so every night before I went to sleep, I made sure that there was no rope in my room lest I be tempted during the night to hang myself from the rafters in my room; and I stopped from going out shooting lest I be tempted to put a quick end to my life and to my misery.

Like so many people, Tolstoi at that stage of his life lacked the sustaining influence which comes from the conviction that this universe is guided by a benign Intelligence whose infinite love embraces all mankind.

Religion endows us with the conviction that we are not alone in this vast, uncertain universe. Beneath and above the shifting sands of time, the uncertainties that darken our days, and the vicissitudes that cloud our nights is a wise and loving God. This universe is not a tragic expression of meaningless chaos but a marvellous display of orderly cosmos —"The Lord by wisdom hath founded the earth; by understanding hath he established the heavens." Man is not a wisp of smoke from a limitless smouldering, but a child created "a little lower than the angels." Above the many-ness of time stands the one eternal God, with wisdom to guide us, strength to protect us, and love to keep us. His boundless love supports and contains us as a mighty ocean contains and supports the tiny drops of every wave. With a surging fullness he is forever moving toward us, seeking to fill the little creeks and bays of our lives with unlimited resources. This is religion's everlasting diapason, its eternal answer to the enigma of existence. Any man who finds this cosmic sustenance can walk the highways of life without the fatigue of pessimism and the weight of morbid fears.

Herein lies the answer to the neurotic fear of death that plagues so many of our lives. Let us face the fear that the atomic bomb has aroused with the faith that we can never travel beyond the arms of the Divine. Death is inevitable. It is a democracy for all of the people, not an aristocracy for some of the people—kings die and beggars die; young men die and old men die; learned men die and ignorant men die. We need not fear it. The God who brought our whirling planet from primal vapour and has led the human pilgrimage for lo these many centuries can most assuredly lead us through death's dark night into the bright daybreak of eternal life. His will is too perfect and his purposes are too extensive to be contained in the limited receptacle of time and the narrow walls of earth. Death is not the ultimate evil; the ultimate evil is to be outside God's love. We need not join the mad rush to purchase an earthly fallout shelter. God is our eternal fallout shelter.

Jesus knew that nothing could separate man from the love of God. Listen to his majestic words:

Fear them not therefore: for there is nothing covered, that shall not be revealed; and hid, that shall not be known. . . . And fear not them which kill the body, but are not able to kill the soul: but rather fear him which is able to destroy both soul and body in hell. Are not two sparrows sold for a farthing? and one of them shall not fall on the ground without your Father. But the very hairs of your head are all numbered. Fear ye not therefore, ye are of more value than many sparrows.

Man, for Jesus, is not mere flotsam and jetsam in the river of life, but he is a child of God. Is it not unreasonable to assume that God, whose creative activity is expressed in an awareness of a sparrow's fall and the number of hairs on a man's head, excludes from his encompassing love the life of man itself? The confidence that God is mindful of the individual is of tremendous value in dealing with the disease of fear, for it gives us a sense of worth, of belonging, and of at-homeness in the universe.

One of the most dedicated participants in the bus protest in Montgomery, Alabama, was an elderly Negro whom we affectionately called Mother Pollard. Although poverty-stricken and uneducated, she was amazingly intelligent and possessed a deep understanding of the meaning of the movement. After having walked for several weeks, she was asked if she were tired. With ungrammatical profundity, she answered, "My feets is tired, but my soul is rested."

On a particular Monday evening, following a tension-packed week which included being arrested and receiving numerous threatening telephone calls, I spoke at a mass meeting. I attempted to convey an overt impression of strength and courage, although I was inwardly depressed and fear-stricken. At the end of the meeting, Mother Pollard came to the front of the church and said, "Come here, son." I immediately went to her and hugged her affectionately. "Something is wrong with you," she said. "You didn't talk strong tonight." Seeking further to disguise my fears, I retorted, "Oh, no, Mother Pollard, nothing is wrong. I am feeling as fine as ever." But her insight was discerning. "Now you can't fool me," she said. "I knows something is wrong. Is it that we ain't doing things to please you? Or is it that the white folks is bothering you?" Before I could respond, she looked directly into my eyes and said, "I don told you we is with you all the way." Then her face became radiant and she said in words of quiet certainty, "But even if we ain't with you, God's gonna take care of you." As she spoke these consoling words, everything in me quivered and quickened with the pulsing tremor of raw energy.

Since that dreary night in 1956, Mother Pollard has passed on to glory and I have known very few quiet days. I have been tortured without and tormented within by the raging fires of tribulation. I have been forced to muster what strength and courage I have to withstand howling winds of pain and jostling storms of adversity. But as the years have unfolded the eloquently simple words of Mother Pollard have come back again and again to give light and peace and guidance to my troubled soul. "God's gonna take care of you."

This faith transforms the whirlwind of despair into a warm and reviving breeze of hope. The words of a motto which a generation ago were commonly found on the wall in the homes of devout persons need to be etched on our hearts:

> Fear knocked at the door.
> Faith answered.
> There was no one there.

CHAPTER THIRTEEN

The answer to a perplexing question

Why could not we cast him out?
                    Matthew 17:19

Human life through the centuries has been characterized by man's persistent efforts to remove evil from the earth. Seldom has man thoroughly adjusted himself to evil, for in spite of his rationalizations, compromises, and alibis, he knows the "is" is not the "ought" and the actual is not the possible. Though the evils of sensuality, selfishness, and cruelty often rise aggressively in his soul, something within tells him that they are intruders and reminds him of his higher destiny and more noble allegiance. Man's hankering after the demonic is always disturbed by his longing for the divine. As he seeks to adjust to the demands of time, he knows that eternity is his ultimate habitat. When man comes to himself, he knows that evil is a foreign invader that must be driven from the native soils of his soul before he can achieve moral and spiritual dignity.

But the problem that has always hampered man has been his inability to conquer evil by his own power. In pathetic amazement, he asks, "Why can I not cast it out? Why can I not remove this evil from my life?"

This agonizing, perplexing question recalls an event that occurred immediately after Christ's transfiguration. Coming down from the mountain, Jesus found a small boy who was in wild convulsions. His disciples had tried desperately to cure the unhappy child, but the more they laboured to heal him the more they realized their own inadequacies and the pathetic limitations of their power. When they were about to give up in despair, their Lord appeared on the scene. After the father of the child told Jesus of the failure of the disciples, Jesus "rebuked the devil; and he departed out of him: and the child was cured from that very hour." When the disciples were later alone with their Master, they asked, "Why could not we cast him out?" They wanted an explanation for their obvious limitations. Jesus said their failure was caused by their unbelief: "If ye have faith as a grain of mustard seed, ye shall say unto this mountain, Remove hence to yonder place; and it shall remove; and nothing shall be impossible unto you." They had tried to do by themselves what could be done only after they had so surrendered their natures to God that his strength flowed freely through them.

I

How can evil be cast out? Men have usually pursued two paths to eliminate evil and thereby save the world. The first calls upon man to remove evil through his own power and ingenuity in the strange conviction that by thinking, inventing, and governing, he will at last conquer the nagging forces of evil. Give people a fair chance and a decent education, and they will save themselves. This idea, sweeping across the modern world like a plague, has ushered God out and escorted man in and has substituted human ingenuity for divine guidance. Some people suggest that this concept was introduced during the Renaissance when reason dethroned religion, or later when Darwin's *Origin of Species* replaced belief in creation by the theory of evolution, or when the industrial revolution turned the hearts of men to material comforts and physical conveniences. At any rate, the idea of the adequacy of man to solve the evils of history captured the minds of people, giving rise to the easy optimism of the nineteenth century, the doctrine of inevitable progress, Rousseau's maxim of "the original goodness of human nature," and Condorcet's conviction that by reason alone the whole world would soon be cleansed of crime, poverty, and war.

Armed with this growing faith in the capability of reason and science, modern man set out to change the world. He turned his attention from God and the human soul to the outer world and its possibilities. He observed, analyzed, and explored. The laboratory became man's sanctuary and scientists his priests and prophets. A modern humanist confidently affirmed:

> The future is not with the churches but with the laboratories, not with prophets but with scientists, not with piety but with efficiency. Man is at last becoming aware that he alone is responsible for the realization of the world of his dreams, that he has within himself the power for its achievement.

Man has subpoenaed nature to appear before the judgment seat of scientific investigation. None doubt that man's work in the scientific laboratories has brought unbelievable advances in power and comfort, producing machines that think and gadgets that soar majestically through the skies, stand impressively on the land, and move with stately dignity on the seas.

But in spite of these astounding new scientific developments, the old evils continue and the age of reason has been transformed into an age of terror. Selfishness and hatred have not vanished with an enlargement of our educational system and an extension of our legislative policies. A once optimistic generation now asks in utter bewilderment, "Why could not we cast it out?"

The answer is rather simple: Man by his own power can never cast evil from the world. The humanist's hope is an illusion, based on too great an optimism concerning the inherent goodness of human nature.

I would be the last to condemn the thousands of sincere and dedicated people outside the churches who have laboured unselfishly through various humanitarian movements to cure the world of social evils, for I would rather a man be a committed humanist than an uncommitted Christian. But so many of these dedicated persons, seeking salvation within the human context, have become understandably pessimistic and disillusioned, because their efforts are based on a kind of self-delusion which ignores fundamental facts about our mortal nature.

Nor would I minimize the importance of science and the great contributions which have come in the wake of the Renaissance. These have lifted us from the stagnating valleys of superstition and half-truth to the sunlit mountains of creative analysis and objective appraisal. The unquestioned authority of the church in scientific matters needed to be freed from paralyzing obscurantism, antiquated notions, and shameful inquisitions. But the exalted Renaissance optimism, while attempting to free the mind of man, forgot about man's capacity for sin.

II

The second idea for removing evil from the world stipulates that if man waits submissively upon the Lord, in his own good time God alone will redeem the world. Rooted in a pessimistic doctrine of human nature, this idea, which eliminates completely the capability of sinful man to do anything, was prominent in the Reformation, that great spiritual movement which gave birth to the Protestant concern for moral and spiritual freedom and served as a necessary corrective for a corrupt and stagnant medieval church. The doctrines of justification by faith and the priesthood of all believers are towering principles which we as Protestants must forever affirm, but the Reformation doctrine of human nature overstressed the corruption of man. The Renaissance was too optimistic, and the Reformation too pessimistic. The former so concentrated on the goodness of man that it overlooked his capacity for evil; the latter so concentrated on the wickedness of man that it overlooked his capacity for goodness. While rightly affirming the sinfulness of human nature and man's incapacity to save himself, the Reformation wrongly affirmed that the image of God had been completely erased from man.

This led to the Calvinistic concept of the total depravity of man and to a resurrection of the terrible idea of infant damnation. So depraved is human nature, said the doctrinaire Calvinist, that if a baby dies without baptism he will burn forever in hell. Certainly this carries the idea of man's sinfulness too far.

This lopsided Reformation theology has often emphasized a purely otherworldly religion, which stresses the utter hopelessness of this world and calls upon the individual to concentrate on preparing his soul for the world to come. By ignoring the need for social reform, religion is divorced from the mainstream of human life. A pulpit committee listed as the first essential qualification for a new minister: "He must preach the true gospel and not talk about social issues." This is a blueprint for a dangerously irrelevant church where people assemble to hear only pious platitudes.

By disregarding the fact that the gospel deals with man's body as well as with his soul, such a one-sided emphasis creates a tragic dichotomy between the sacred and the secular. To be worthy of its New Testament origin, the church must seek to transform both individual lives and the social situation that brings to many people anguish of spirit and cruel bondage.

The idea that man expects God to do everything leads inevitably to a callous misuse of prayer. For if God does everything, man then asks him for anything, and God becomes little more than a "cosmic bellhop" who is summoned for every trivial need. Or God is considered so omnipotent and man so powerless that prayer is a substitute for work and intelligence. A man said to me, "I believe in integration, but I know it will not come until God wants it to come. You Negroes should stop protesting and start praying." I am certain we need to pray for God's help and guidance in this integration struggle, but we are gravely misled if we think the struggle will be won only by prayer. God, who gave us minds for thinking and bodies for working, would defeat his own purpose if he permitted us to obtain through prayer what may come through work and intelligence. Prayer is a marvellous and necessary supplement of our feeble efforts, but it is a dangerous substitute. When Moses strove to lead the Israelites to the Promised Land, God made it clear that he would not do for them what they could do for themselves. "And the Lord said unto Moses, Wherefore criest thou unto me? speak unto the children of Israel, that they go forward."

We must pray earnestly for peace, but we must also work vigorously for disarmament and the suspension of weapon testing. We must use our minds as rigorously to plan for peace as we have used them to plan for war. We must pray with unceasing passion for racial justice, but we must also use our minds to develop a programme, organize ourselves into mass nonviolent action, and employ every resource of our bodies and souls to bring an end to racial injustice. We must pray unrelentingly for economic justice, but we must also work diligently to bring into being those social changes that make for a better distribution of wealth within our nation and in the undeveloped countries of the world.

Does not all of this reveal the fallacy of thinking that God will cast evil from the earth, even if man does nothing except to sit complacently by the wayside? No prodigious thunderbolt from heaven will blast away evil. No mighty army of angels will descend to force men to do what their wills resist. The Bible portrays God, not as an omnipotent czar who makes all decisions for his subjects nor as a cosmic tyrant who with gestapo-like methods invades the inner lives of men, but rather as a loving Father who gives to his children such abundant blessings as they may be willing to receive. Always man must do something. "Stand upon thy feet," says God to Ezekiel, "and I will speak unto you." Man is no helpless invalid left in a valley of total depravity until God pulls him out. Man is rather an upstanding human being whose vision has been impaired by the cataracts of sin and whose soul has been weakened by the virus of pride, but there is sufficient vision left for him to lift his eyes unto the hills, and there remains enough of God's image for him to turn his weak and sin-battered life toward the Great Physician, the curer of the ravages of sin.

The real weakness of the idea that God will do everything is its false conception of both God and man. It makes God so absolutely sovereign that man is absolutely helpless. It makes man so absolutely depraved that he can do nothing but wait on God. It sees the world as so contaminated with sin that God totally transcends it and touches it only here and there through a mighty invasion. This view ends up with a God who is a despot and not a Father. It ends up with such a pessimism concerning human nature that it leaves man little more than a helpless worm crawling through the morass of an evil world. But man is neither totally depraved, nor is God an almighty dictator. We must surely affirm the majesty and sovereignty of God, but this should not lead us to believe that God is an Almighty Monarch who will impose his will upon us and deprive us of the freedom to choose what is good or what is not good. He will not thrust himself upon us nor force us to stay home when our minds are bent on journeying to some degrading far country. But he follows us in love, and when we come to ourselves and turn our tired feet back to the Father's house, he stands waiting with outstretched arms of forgiveness.

Therefore we must never feel that God will, through some breath-taking miracle or a wave of the hand, cast evil out of the world. As long as we believe this we will pray unanswerable prayers and ask God to do things that he will never do. The belief that God will do everything for man is as untenable as the belief that man can do everything for himself. It, too, is based on a lack of faith. We must learn that to expect God to do everything while we do nothing is not faith, but superstition.

III

What, then, is the answer to life's perplexing question, "How can evil be cast out of our individual and collective lives?" If the world is not to be purified by God alone nor by man alone, who will do it?

The answer is found in an idea which is distinctly different from the two we have discussed, for neither God nor man will individually bring the world's salvation. Rather, both man and God, made one in a marvellous unity of purpose through an overflowing love as the free gift of himself on the part of God and by perfect obedience and receptivity on the part of man, can transform the old into the new and drive out the deadly cancer of sin.

The principle which opens the door for God to work through man is faith. This is what the disciples lacked when they desperately tried to remove the nagging evil from the body of the sick child. Jesus reminded them that they had been attempting to do by themselves what could be done only when their lives were open receptacles, as it were, into which God's strength could be freely poured.

Two types of faith in God are clearly set forth in the Scriptures. One may be called the mind's faith, wherein the intellect assents to a belief that God exists. The other may be referred to as the heart's faith, whereby the whole man is involved in a trusting act of self-surrender. To know God, a man must possess this latter type of faith, for the mind's faith is directed toward a theory, but the heart's faith is centred in a Person. Gabriel Marcel claims that faith is *believing in*, not *believing that*. It is "opening a credit; which puts me at the disposal of the one in whom I believe." When I believe, he says, "I rally to with that sort of interior gathering of oneself which the act of rallying implies." Faith is the opening of all sides and at every level of one's life to the divine inflow.

This is what the Apostle Paul emphasized in his doctrine of salvation by faith. For him, faith is man's capacity to accept God's willingness through Christ to rescue us from the bondage of sin. In his magnanimous love, God freely offers to do for us what we cannot do for ourselves. Our humble and openhearted acceptance is faith. So by faith we are saved. Man filled with God and God operating through man bring unbelievable changes in our individual and social lives.

Social evils have trapped multitudes of men in a dark and murky corridor where there is no exit sign and plunged others into a dark abyss of psychological fatalism. These deadly, paralyzing evils can be removed by a humanity perfectly united through obedience with God. Moral victory will come as God fills man and man opens his life by faith to God, even as the gulf opens to the overflowing waters of the river. Racial justice, a genuine possibility in our nation and in the world, will come neither by our frail and often misguided efforts nor by God imposing his will on wayward men, but when enough people open their lives to God and allow him to pour his triumphant, divine energy into their souls. Our age-old and noble dream of a world of peace may yet become a reality, but it will come neither by man working alone nor by God destroying the wicked schemes of men, but when men so open their lives to God that he may fill them with love, mutual respect, understanding, and goodwill. Social salvation will come only through man's willing acceptance of God's mighty gift.

Let me apply what I have been saying to our personal lives. Many of you know what it means to struggle with sin. Year by year you were aware that a terrible sin—slavery to drink, perhaps, or untruthfulness, impurity, selfishness—was taking possession of your life. As the years unfolded and the vice widened its landmarks on your soul, you knew that it was an unnatural intruder. You may have thought, "One day I shall drive this evil out. I know it is destroying my character and embarrassing my family." At last you determined to purge yourself of the evil by making a New Year's resolution. Do you remember your surprise and disappointment when you discovered, three hundred and sixty-five days later, that your most sincere efforts had not banished the old habit from your life? In complete amazement you asked, "Why could not I cast it out?"

In despair you decided to take your problem to God, but instead of asking him to work through you, you said, "God, you must solve this problem for me. I can't do anything about it." But days and months later the evil was still with you. God would not cast it out, for he never removes sin without the cordial co-operation of the sinner. No problem is solved when we idly wait for God to undertake full responsibility.

One cannot remove an evil habit by mere resolution nor by simply calling on God to do the job, but only as he surrenders himself and becomes an instrument of God. We shall be delivered from the accumulated weight of evil only when we permit the energy of God to come into our souls.

God has promised to co-operate with us when we seek to cast evil from our lives and become true children of his divine will. "If any one is in Christ," says Paul, "he is a new creation; the old has passed away, behold, the new has come." If any man is in Christ, he is a new person, his old self has gone, and he becomes a divinely transformed son of God.

One of the great glories of the gospel is that Christ has transformed nameless prodigals. He turned a Simon of sand into a Peter of rock. He changed a persecuting Saul into an Apostle Paul. He converted a lust-feasted Augustine into a St. Augustine. The measured words of Leo Tolstoi's confession in *My Religion* reflect an experience many have shared:

> Five years ago faith came to me; I believed in the doctrine of Jesus, and my whole life underwent a sudden transformation. What I had once wished for I wished for no longer, and I began to desire what I had never desired before. What had once appeared to me right now became wrong, and the wrong of the past I beheld as right. . . . My life and my desires were completely changed; good and evil interchanged meanings.

Herein we find the answer to a perplexing question. Evil can be cast out, not by man alone nor by a dictatorial God who invades our lives, but when we open the door and invite God through Christ to enter. "Behold, I stand at the door, and knock: if any man hear my voice, and open the door, I will come in to him, and will sup with him, and he with me." God is too courteous to break open the door, but when we open it in faith believing, a divine and human confrontation will transform our sin-ruined lives into radiant personalities.

CHAPTER FOURTEEN

Paul's letter to American Christians

I would like to share with you an imaginary letter from the pen of the Apostle Paul. The postmark reveals that it comes from the port city of Troas. On opening the letter I discovered that it was written in Greek rather than in English. After working assiduously with the translation for several weeks, I think I have now deciphered its true meaning. If the content of this epistle sounds strangely Kingian instead of Paulinian, attribute it to my lack of complete objectivity rather than Paul's lack of clarity. Here is the letter as it stands before me.

Paul, called to be an apostle of Jesus Christ by the will of God, to you who are in America, grace be unto you, and peace, from God our Father, through our Lord and Saviour, Jesus Christ.

For many years I have longed to see you. I have heard so much about you and of what you are doing. News has come to me regarding the fascinating and astounding advances that you have made in the scientific realm. I have learned of your dashing subways and flashing aeroplanes. Through your scientific genius you have dwarfed distance and placed time in chains. You have made it possible to eat breakfast in Paris, France, and lunch in New York City. I have also heard of your skyscraper buildings with their prodigious towers rising heavenward. I am told of your great medical advances and the curing of many dread plagues and diseases, thereby prolonging your lives and offering greater security and physical well-being. All of that is marvellous. You can do so many things in your day that I could not do in the Greco-Roman world of my day. You travel distances in a single day that in my generation required three months. That is wonderful. What tremendous strides in the areas of scientific and technological development you have made!

But, America, I wonder whether your moral and spiritual progress has been commensurate with your scientific progress. It appears to me that your moral progress lags behind your scientific progress, your mentality outdistances your morality, and your civilization outshines your culture. How much of your modern life can be summarized in the words of your poet Thoreau: "Improved means to an unimproved end." Through your scientific genius you have made of the world a neighbourhood, but you have failed to employ your moral and spiritual genius to make of it a brotherhood. So, America, the atomic bomb you have to fear today is not merely that deadly weapon which can be dropped from an aeroplane on the heads of millions of people, but that atomic bomb which lies in the hearts of men, capable of exploding into the most staggering hate and the most devastating selfishness. Therefore I would urge you to keep your moral advances abreast of your scientific advances.

I find it necessary to remind you of the responsibility laid upon you to represent the ethical principles of Christianity amid a time that popularly disregards them. That was a task laid on me. I understand that there are many Christians in America who give their ultimate allegiance to man-made systems and customs. They are afraid to be different. Their great concern is to be accepted socially. They live by some such principle as this: "Everybody is doing it, so it must be all right." For so many of you morality merely reflects group consensus. In your modern sociological lingo, the mores are accepted as the right ways. You have unconsciously come to believe that what is right is determined by Gallup polls.

American Christians, I must say to you what I wrote to the Roman Christians years ago: "Be not conformed to this world: but be ye transformed by the renewing of your mind." You have a duel citizenry. You live both in time and eternity. Your highest loyalty is to God, and not to the mores or the folkways, the state or the nation, or any man-made institution. If any earthly institution or custom conflicts with God's will, it is your Christian duty to oppose it. You must never allow the transitory, evanescent demands of man-made institutions to take precedence over the eternal demands of the Almighty God. In a time when men are surrendering the high values of the faith you must cling to them, and despite the pressure of an alien generation preserve them for children yet unborn. You must be willing to challenge unjust mores, to champion unpopular causes, and to buck the status quo. You are called to be the salt of the earth. You are to be the light of the world. You are to be that vitally active leaven in the lump of the nation.

I understand that you have an economic system in America known as capitalism, through which you have accomplished wonders. You have become the richest nation in the world, and you have built the greatest system of production that history has ever known. All of this is marvellous. But, Americans, there is the danger that you will misuse your capitalism. I still contend that the love of money is the root of much evil and may cause a man to become a gross materialist. I am afraid that many among you are more concerned in making money than in accumulating spiritual treasures.

The misuse of capitalism may also lead to tragic exploitation. This has so often happened in your nation. I am told that one tenth of ·1 per cent of the population controls more than 40 per cent of the wealth. America, how often have you taken necessities from the masses and given luxuries to the classes. If you are to be a truly Christian nation, you must solve this problem. You cannot solve it by turning to Communism, for Communism is based on an ethical relativism, a metaphysical materialism, a crippling totalitarianism, and a withdrawal of basic freedom that no Christian can accept. But you can work within the framework of democracy to bring about a better distribution of wealth. You must use your powerful economic resources to eliminate poverty from the earth. God never intended one people to live in superfluous and inordinate wealth, while others know only deadening poverty. God wants all of his children to have the basic necessities of life, and he has left in this universe "enough and to spare" for that purpose.

I would that I might be with you in person, so that I could say to you face to face what I am forced to put down in writing. Oh, how I long to share your fellowship!

Let me say something about the church. Americans, I must remind you, as I have told so many others, that the church is the Body of Christ. When the church is true to its nature, it knows neither division nor disunity. I am told that within American Protestantism there are more than two hundred and fifty denominations. The tragedy is not merely that you have such a multiplicity of denominations, but that many groups claim to possess absolute truth. Such narrow sectarianism destroys the unity of the Body of Christ. God is neither Baptist, Methodist, Presbyterian, nor Episcopalian. God transcends our denominations. If you are to be true witnesses for Christ, you must come to know this, America.

I am happy to hear that there is a growing concern for church unity and ecumenicity in America. I have word that you have organized a National Council of Churches and that most of your major denominations are affiliated with the World Council of Churches. All of this is marvellous. Continue to follow this creative path. Keep these church councils alive and continue to give them your unstinted support. I have the encouraging news that there has been some recent dialogue between Roman Catholics and Protestants. I am told that several Protestant churchmen from your nation accepted Pope John's invitation to be observers at a recent ecumenical council in Rome. This is both a significant and healthy sign. I hope it is the beginning of a development that will bring all Christians closer and closer together.

Another thing that disturbs me about the American church is that you have a white church and a Negro church. How can segregation exist in the true Body of Christ? I am told that there is more integration within the entertaining world and other secular agencies than there is in the Christian church. How appalling this is!

I understand that there are Christians among you who try to find biblical bases to justify segregation and argue that the Negro is inferior by nature. Oh, my friends, this is blasphemy and against everything that the Christian religion stands for. I must repeat what I have said to many Christians before, that in Christ "there is neither Jew nor Greek, there is neither bond nor free, there is neither male nor female: for ye are all one in Christ Jesus." Moreover, I must reiterate the words I uttered on Mars Hill: "God that made the world and all things therein . . . hath made of one blood all nations of men for to dwell on all the face of the earth."

So, Americans, I must urge you to be rid of every aspect of segregation. Segregation is a blatant denial of the unity which we have in Christ. It substitutes an "I-it" relationship for the "I-thou" relationship, and relegates persons to the status of things. It scars the soul and degrades the personality. It inflicts the segregated with a false sense of inferiority, while confirming the segregator in a false estimate of his own superiority. It destroys community and makes brotherhood impossible. The underlying philosophy of Christianity is diametrically opposed to the underlying philosophy of racial segregation.

I praise your Supreme Court for rendering a historic desegregation decision and also persons of goodwill who have accepted this as a great moral victory, but I understand that some brothers have risen up in open defiance and that their legislative halls ring loud with such words as "nullification" and "interposition." Because these brothers have lost the true meaning of democracy and Christianity, I urge each of you to plead patiently with them. With understanding and goodwill, you are obligated to seek to change their attitudes. Let them know that in standing against integration, they are not only opposing the noble precepts of your democracy, but also the eternal edicts of God himself.

I hope the churches of America will play a significant role in conquering segregation. It has always been the responsibility of the church to broaden horizons and challenge the status quo. The church must move out into the arena of social action. First, you must see that the church removes the yoke of segregation from its own body. Then you must seek to make the church increasingly active in social action outside its doors. It must seek to keep channels of communication open between the races. It must take an active stand against the injustices which Negroes confront in housing, education, police protection, and in city and state courts. It must exert its influence in the area of economic justice. As guardian of the moral and spiritual life of the community the church cannot look with indifference upon these glaring evils. If you as Christians will accept the challenge with devotion and valour, you will lead the misguided men of your nation from the darkness of falsehood and fear to the light of truth and love.

May I say just a word to those of you who are the victims of the evil system of segregation. You must continue to work passionately and vigorously for your God-given and constitutional rights. It would be both cowardly and immoral for you patiently to accept injustice. You cannot in good conscience sell your birthright of freedom for a mess of segregated pottage. But as you continue your righteous protest always be sure that you struggle with Christian methods and Christian weapons. Be sure that the means you employ are as pure as the end you seek. Never succumb to the temptation of becoming bitter. As you press on for justice, be sure to move with dignity and discipline, using love as your chief weapon. Let no man pull you so low that you hate him. Always avoid violence. If you sow the seeds of violence in your struggle, unborn generations will reap the whirlwind of social disintegration.

In your struggle for justice, let your oppressor know that you have neither a desire to defeat him nor a desire to get even with him for injustices that he has heaped upon you. Let him know that the festering sore of segregation debilitates the white man as well as the Negro. By having this attitude, you will keep your struggle on high Christian levels.

Many persons realize the urgency of eradicating the evil of segregation. Many Negroes will devote their lives to the cause of freedom, and many white persons of goodwill and strong moral sensitivity will dare to speak for justice. Honesty impels me to admit that such a stand requires a willingness to suffer and sacrifice. Do not despair if you are condemned and persecuted for righteousness' sake. When you testify for truth and justice, you are liable to scorn. Often you will be called an impractical idealist or a dangerous radical. You may even be called a Communist merely because you believe in the brotherhood of man. Sometimes you may be put in jail. If such is the case, you must honourably grace the jail with your presence. It may mean losing a job or social standing with your particular group. Even if physical death is the price that some must pay to free their children from psychological death, then nothing could be more Christian. Do not worry about persecution, American Christians; you must accept this when you stand up for a great principle. I speak with some authority, for my life was a continual round of persecutions. After my conversion I was rejected by the disciples at Jerusalem. Later I was tried for heresy at Jerusalem. I was jailed at Philippi, beaten at Thessalonica, mobbed at Ephesus, and depressed at Athens. I came away from each of these experiences more persuaded than ever that "neither death, nor life, nor angels, nor principalities . . . nor things present, nor things to come . . . shall . . . separate us from the love of God, which is in Christ Jesus our Lord." The end of life is not to be happy nor to achieve pleasure and avoid pain, but to do the will of God, come what may. I have nothing but praise for those of you who have already stood unflinchingly before threats and intimidation, inconvenience and unpopularity, arrest and physical violence, to declare the doctrine of the Fatherhood of God and the brotherhood of man. For such noble servants of God there is the consolation of the words of Jesus: "Blessed are ye, when men shall revile you, and persecute you, and shall say all manner of evil against you falsely, for my sake. Rejoice, and be exceeding glad: for great is your reward in heaven: for so persecuted they the prophets which were before you."

I must bring my writing to a close. Silas is waiting to deliver this letter, and I must take leave for Macedonia, from which an urgent plea has come requesting help. But before leaving, I must say to you, as I said to the Church of Corinth, that love is the most durable power in the world. Throughout the centuries men have sought to discover the highest good. This has been the chief quest of ethical philosophy. This was one of the big questions of Greek philosophy. The Epicureans and the Stoics sought to answer it; Plato and Aristotle sought to answer it. What is the *summum bonum* of life? I think I have found the answer, America. I have discovered that the highest good is love. This principle is at the centre of the cosmos. It is the great unifying force of life. God is love. He who loves has discovered the clue to the meaning of ultimate reality; he who hates stands in immediate candidacy for nonbeing.

American Christians, you may master the intricacies of the English language and you may possess the eloquence of articulate speech; but even though you speak with the tongues of men and of angels, and have not love, you are like sounding brass or a tinkling cymbal.

You may have the gift of scientific prediction and understand the behaviour of molecules, you may break into the storehouse of nature and bring forth many new insights, you may ascend to the heights of academic achievement, so that you have all knowledge, and you may boast of your great institutions of learning and the boundless extent of your degrees; but, devoid of love, all of these mean absolutely nothing.

But even more, Americans, you may give your goods to feed the poor, you may bestow great gifts to charity, and you may tower high in philanthropy, but if you have not love, your charity means nothing. You may even give your body to be burned, and die the death of a martyr, and your spilled blood may be a symbol of honour for generations yet unborn, and thousands may praise you as one of history's supreme heroes; but even so, if you have not love, your blood is spilled in vain. You must come to see that a man may be self-centred in his self-denial and self-righteous in his self-sacrifice. His generosity may feed his ego and his piety his pride. Without love, benevolence becomes egotism and martyrdom becomes spiritual pride.

The greatest of all virtues is love. Here we find the true meaning of the Christian faith and of the cross. Calvary is a telescope through which we look into the long vista of eternity and see the love of God breaking into time. Out of the hugeness of his generosity God allowed his only-begotten Son to die that we may live. By uniting yourselves with Christ and your brothers through love you will be able to matriculate in the university of eternal life. In a world depending on force, coercive tyranny, and bloody violence, you are challenged to follow the way of love. You will then discover that unarmed love is the most powerful force in all the world.

I must say good-bye. Extend my warmest greeting to all the saints in the household of Christ. Be of good comfort; be of one mind; and live in peace.

It is improbable that I will see you in America, but I will meet you in God's eternity. And now unto him who is able to keep us from falling, and lift us from the dark valley of despair to the bright mountain of hope, from the midnight of desperation to the daybreak of joy, to him be power and authority, for ever and ever. Amen.

CHAPTER FIFTEEN

Pilgrimage to nonviolence

In my senior year in theological seminary, I engaged in the
exciting reading of various theological theories. Having been
raised in a rather strict fundamentalist tradition, I was occa-
sionally shocked when my intellectual journey carried me
through new and sometimes complex doctrinal lands, but
the pilgrimage was always stimulating, gave me a new
appreciation for objective appraisal and critical analysis,
and knocked me out of my dogmatic slumber.

Liberalism provided me with an intellectual satisfaction
that I had never found in fundamentalism. I became so
enamoured of the insights of liberalism that I almost fell
into the trap of accepting uncritically everything it encompassed. I was absolutely convinced of the natural goodness
of man and the natural power of human reason.

I

A basic change in my thinking came when I began to question some of the theories that had been associated with
so-called liberal theology. Of course, there are aspects of
liberalism that I hope to cherish always: its devotion to the
search for truth, its insistence on an open and analytical
mind, and its refusal to abandon the best lights of reason.
The contribution of liberalism to the philological-historical
criticism of biblical literature has been of immeasurable
value and should be defended with religious and scientific
passion.

But I began to question the liberal doctrine of man. The

more I observed the tragedies of history and man's shameful inclination to choose the low road, the more I came to see the depths and strength of sin. My reading of the works of Reinhold Niebuhr made me aware of the complexity of human motives and the reality of sin on every level of man's existence. Moreover, I came to recognize the complexity of man's social involvement and the glaring reality of collective evil. I realized that liberalism had been all too sentimental concerning human nature and that it leaned toward a false idealism.

I also came to see that the superficial optimism of liberalism concerning human nature overlooked the fact that reason is darkened by sin. The more I thought about human nature, the more I saw how our tragic inclination for sin encourages us to rationalize our actions. Liberalism failed to show that reason by itself is little more than an instrument to justify man's defensive ways of thinking. Reason, devoid of the purifying power of faith, can never free itself from distortions and rationalizations.

Although I rejected some aspects of liberalism, I never came to an all-out acceptance of neo-orthodoxy. While I saw neo-orthodoxy as a helpful corrective for a sentimental liberalism, I felt that it did not provide an adequate answer to basic questions. If liberalism was too optimistic concerning human nature, neo-orthodoxy was too pessimistic. Not only on the question of man, but also on other vital issues, the revolt of neo-orthodoxy went too far. In its attempt to preserve the transcendence of God, which had been neglected by an overstress of his immanence in liberalism, neo-orthodoxy went to the extreme of stressing a God who was hidden, unknown, and "wholly other." In its revolt against overemphasis on the power of reason in liberalism, neo-orthodoxy fell into a mood of antirationalism and semifundamentalism, stressing a narrow uncritical biblicism. This approach, I felt, was inadequate both for the church and for personal life.

So although liberalism left me unsatisfied on the question of the nature of man, I found no refuge in neo-orthodoxy. I am now convinced that the truth about man is found neither in liberalism nor in neo-orthodoxy. Each represents a partial truth. A large segment of Protestant liberalism defined man only in terms of his essential nature, his capacity for good; neo-orthodoxy tended to define man only in terms of his existential nature, his capacity for evil. An adequate understanding of man is found neither in the thesis of liberalism nor in the antithesis of neo-orthodoxy, but in a synthesis which reconciles the truths of both.

During the intervening years I have gained a new appreciation for the philosophy of existentialism. My first contact with this philosophy came through my reading of Kierkegaard and Nietzsche. Later I turned to a study of Jaspers, Heidegger, and Sartre. These thinkers stimulated my thinking; while questioning each, I nevertheless learned a great deal through a study of them. When I finally engaged in a serious study of the writings of Paul Tillich, I became convinced that existentialism, in spite of the fact that it had become all too fashionable, had grasped certain basic truths about man and his condition that could not be permanently overlooked.

An understanding of the "finite freedom" of man is one of the permanent contributions of existentialism, and its perception of the anxiety and conflict produced in man's personal and social life by the perilous and ambiguous structure of existence is especially meaningful for our time. A common denominator in atheistic or theistic existentialism is that man's existential situation is estranged from his essential nature. In their revolt against Hegel's essentialism, all existentialists contend that the world is fragmented. History is a series of unreconciled conflicts, and man's existence is filled with anxiety and threatened with meaninglessness. While the ultimate Christian answer is not found in any of these existential assertions, there is much here by which the theologian may describe the true state of man's existence.

Although most of my formal study has been in systematic theology and philosophy, I have become more and more interested in social ethics. During my early teens I was deeply concerned by the problem of racial injustice. I considered segregation both rationally inexplicable and morally unjustifiable. I could never accept my having to sit in the back of a bus or in the segregated section of a train. The first time that I was seated behind a curtain in a dining-car I felt as though the curtain had been dropped on my selfhood. I also learned that the inseparable twin of racial injustice is economic injustice. I saw how the systems of segregation exploited both the Negro and the poor whites. These early experiences made me deeply conscious of the varieties of injustice in our society.

I I

Not until I entered theological seminary, however, did I begin a serious intellectual quest for a method that would eliminate social evil. I was immediately influenced by the social gospel. In the early 1950s I read Walter Rauschenbusch's *Christianity and the Social Crisis*, a book which left an indelible imprint on my thinking. Of course, there were points at which I differed with Rauschenbusch. I felt that he was a victim of the nineteenth-century "cult of inevitable progress," which led him to an unwarranted optimism concerning human nature. Moreover, he came perilously close to identifying the Kingdom of God with a particular social and economic system, a temptation to which the church must never surrender. But in spite of these shortcomings, Rauschenbusch gave to American Protestantism a sense of social responsibility that it should never lose. The gospel at its best deals with the whole man, not only his soul but also his body, not only his spiritual well-being but also his material well-being. A religion that professes a concern for the souls of men and is not equally concerned about the slums that damn them, the economic conditions that strangle them, and the social conditions that cripple them, is a spiritually moribund religion.

After reading Rauschenbusch, I turned to a serious study of the social and ethical theories of the great philosophers. During this period I had almost despaired of the power of love to solve social problems. The turn-the-other-cheek and the love-your-enemies philosophies are valid, I felt, only when individuals are in conflict with other individuals; when racial groups and nations are in conflict, a more realistic approach is necessary.

Then I was introduced to the life and teachings of Mahatma Gandhi. As I read his works I became deeply fascinated by his campaigns of nonviolent resistance. The whole Gandhian concept of *satyagraha* (*satya* is truth which equals love and *graha* is force; *satyagraha* thus means truth-force or love-force) was profoundly significant to me. As I delved deeper into the philosophy of Gandhi, my scepticism concerning the power of love gradually diminished, and I came to see for the first time that the Christian doctrine of love, operating through the Gandhian method of non-violence, is one of the most potent weapons available to an oppressed people in their struggle for freedom. At that time, however, I acquired only an intellectual understanding and appreciation of the position, and I had no firm determination to organize it in a socially effective situation.

When I was in Montgomery, Alabama, as a pastor in 1954, I had not the slightest idea that I would later become involved in a crisis in which nonviolent resistance would be applicable. After I had lived in the community about a year, the bus boycott began. The Negro people of Montgomery, exhausted by the humiliating experiences that they had constantly faced on the buses, expressed in a massive act of non-co-operation their determination to be free. They came to see that it was ultimately more honourable to walk the streets in dignity than to ride the buses in humiliation. At the beginning of the protest, the people called on me to serve as their spokesman. In accepting this responsibility, my mind, consciously or unconsciously, was driven back to the Sermon on the Mount and the Gandhian method of non-violent resistance. This principle became the guiding light of our movement. Christ furnished the spirit and motivation and Gandhi furnished the method.

The experience in Montgomery did more to clarify my thinking in regard to the question of nonviolence than all of the books that I had read. As the days unfolded, I became more and more convinced of the power of nonviolence.

Nonviolence became more than a method to which I gave intellectual assent; it became a commitment to a way of life. Many issues I had not cleared up intellectually concerning nonviolence were now resolved within the sphere of practical action.

My privilege of travelling to India had a great impact on me personally, for it was invigorating to see firsthand the amazing results of a nonviolent struggle to achieve independence. The aftermath of hatred and bitterness that usually follows a violent campaign was found nowhere in India, and a mutual friendship, based on complete equality, existed between the Indian and British people within the Commonwealth.

I would not wish to give the impression that nonviolence will accomplish miracles overnight. Men are not easily moved from their mental ruts or purged of their prejudiced and irrational feelings. When the underprivileged demand freedom, the privileged at first react with bitterness and resistance. Even when the demands are couched in nonviolent terms, the initial response is substantially the same. I am sure that many of our white brothers in Montgomery and throughout the South are still bitter toward the Negro leaders, even though these leaders have sought to follow a way of love and nonviolence. But the nonviolent approach does something to the hearts and souls of those committed to it. It gives them new self-respect. It calls up resources of strength and courage that they did not know they had. Finally, it so stirs the conscience of the opponent that reconciliation becomes a reality.

III

More recently I have come to see the need for the method of nonviolence in international relations. Although I was not yet convinced of its efficacy in conflicts between nations, I felt that while war could never be a positive good, it could serve as a negative good by preventing the spread and growth of an evil force. War, horrible as it is, might be preferable to surrender to a totalitarian system. But I now believe that the potential destructiveness of modern weapons totally rules out the possibility of war ever again achieving a negative good. If we assume that mankind has a right to survive, then we must find an alternative to war and destruction. In our day of space vehicles and guided ballistic missiles, the choice is either nonviolence or nonexistence.

I am no doctrinaire pacifist, but I have tried to embrace a realistic pacifism which finds the pacifist position as the lesser evil in the circumstances. I do not claim to be free from the moral dilemmas that the Christian nonpacifist confronts, but I am convinced that the church cannot be silent while mankind faces the threat of nuclear annihilation. If the church is true to her mission, she must call for an end to the arms race.

Some of my personal sufferings over the last few years have also served to shape my thinking. I always hesitate to mention these experiences for fear of conveying the wrong impression. A person who constantly calls attention to his trials and sufferings is in danger of developing a martyr complex and impressing others that he is consciously seeking sympathy. It is possible for one to be self-centred in his self-sacrifice. But I feel somewhat justified in mentioning them in this essay because of the influence they have had upon my thought.

Due to my involvement in the struggle for the freedom of my people, I have known very few quiet days in the last few years. I have been imprisoned in Alabama and Georgia jails twelve times. My home has been bombed twice. A day seldom passes that my family and I are not the recipients of threats of death. I have been the victim of a near-fatal stabbing. So in a real sense I have been battered by the storms of persecution. I must admit that at times I have felt that I could no longer bear such a heavy burden, and have been tempted to retreat to a more quiet and serene life. But every time such a temptation appeared, something came to strengthen and sustain my determination. I have learned now that the Master's burden is light precisely when we take his yoke upon us.

My personal trials have also taught me the value of unmerited suffering. As my sufferings mounted I soon realized that there were two ways in which I could respond to my situation—either to react with bitterness or seek to transform the suffering into a creative force. I decided to follow the latter course. Recognizing the necessity for suffering, I have tried to make of it a virtue. If only to save myself from bitterness, I have attempted to see my personal ordeals as an opportunity to transfigure myself and heal the people involved in the tragic situation which now obtains. I have lived these last few years with the conviction that unearned suffering is redemptive. There are some who still find the cross a stumbling block, others consider it foolishness, but I am more convinced than ever before that it is the power of God unto social and individual salvation. So like the Apostle Paul I can now humbly, yet proudly, say, "I bear in my body the marks of the Lord Jesus."

The agonizing moments through which I have passed during the last few years have also drawn me closer to God. More than ever before I am convinced of the reality of a personal God. True, I have always believed in the personality of God. But in the past the idea of a personal God was little more than a metaphysical category that I found theologically and philosophically satisfying. Now it is a living reality that has been validated in the experiences of everyday life. God has been profoundly real to me in recent years. In the midst of outer dangers I have felt an inner calm. In the midst of lonely days and dreary nights I have heard an inner voice saying, "Lo, I will be with you." When the chains of fear and the manacles of frustration have all but stymied my efforts, I have felt the power of God transforming the fatigue of despair into the buoyancy of hope. I am convinced that the universe is under the control of a loving purpose, and that in the struggle for righteousness man has cosmic companionship. Behind the harsh appearances of the world there is a benign power. To say that this God is personal is not to make him a finite object besides other objects or attribute to him the limitations of human personality; it is to take what is finest and noblest in our consciousness and affirm its perfect existence in him. It is certainly true that human personality is limited, but personality as such involves no necessary limitations. It means simply self-consciousness and self-direction. So in the truest sense of the word, God is a living God. In him there is feeling and will, responsive to the deepest yearnings of the human heart: *this* God both evokes and answers prayer.

The past decade has been a most exciting one. In spite of the tensions and uncertainties of this period something profoundly meaningful is taking place. Old systems of exploitation and oppression are passing away; new systems of justice and equality are being born. In a real sense this is a great time to be alive. Therefore, I am not yet discouraged about the future. Granted that the easygoing optimism of yesterday is impossible. Granted that we face a world crisis which leaves us standing so often amid the surging murmur of life's restless sea. But every crisis has both its dangers and its opportunities. It can spell either salvation or doom. In a dark, confused world the Kingdom of God may yet reign in the hearts of men.

Sources

I. A TOUGH MIND AND A TENDER HEART

Page Line
15   1   John 18:11.

II. TRANSFORMED NON-CONFORMIST

18   9   Philippians 3:20 (MOFFATT).
18   33   Luke 12:15.
18   37   Matthew 5:28.
19   3   Matthew 5:10.
19   6   Matthew 21:31.
19   10   Matthew 25:40.
19   14   Matthew 5:44.
19   24   *Hyperion*, Bk. IV, Chap. 7.
20   36   *Writings*. Vol. X, p. 173.
22   28   "Stanzas on Freedom" (extract).
23   7   Romans 12:2.
24   19   Daniel 3:17-18.
24   22   "The Declaration of Independence" (extract).
24   30   Matthew 26:52
25   14   William Hamilton Nelson, *Tinker and Thinker:*
                 John Bunyan (1928).

IV. LOVE IN ACTION

37   32   Matthew 18:21.
39   25   Exodus 21:23-24
43   28   Sonnet XCIV (extract).
44   14   Romans 10:2.
45   18   John 3:19.

V. LOVING YOUR ENEMIES

49   19   *Metamorphoses*, Bk. VII (*Video meliora, proboque;*
                 deteriora sequor).

Page Line
49   23   Romans 7:19.
55   25   Hymn by Isaac Watts (extract).
55   30   Extract from "No East or West," *Selected Poems of John Oxenham*, ed. by Charles L. Wallis. Reprinted by permission of Harper & Row, Publishers.

VI. A KNOCK AT MIDNIGHT

60   4   *Essays on Freedom and Power* (1948).
64   25   Quoted in *Deep River* by Howard Thurman (1955).
64   38   *Ibid.*
66   20   Psalm 30:5.

VII. THE MAN WHO WAS A FOOL

69   1   Matthew 6:8.
69   5   Matthew 6:33.
73   17   Psalm 46:1.
74   9   Abraham Mitrie Rihbany, *Wise Men from the East and from the West* (1922), p. 137.
74   35   Luke 12:15.
74   37   Luke 12:33.

VIII. THE DEATH OF EVIL UPON THE SEASHORE

77   28   "The Battle-Field" (extract).
77   29   *The French Revolution*, Vol. I, Bk. III.
78   34   Hebrews 12:11.
79   3   *Hamlet*, Act V, Scene II.
79   6   "The Present Crisis" (extract).
79   9   *In Memoriam* (extract).
79   28   Speech at the Mansion House, November 10, 1942.
80   24   Letter to John Holmes, April 22, 1820.
80   39   Annual Message to Congress, December 1, 1820.
81   7   *Douglass' Monthly*, January 1, 1863, p. 1.
83   10   Luke 17:21 (RSV).
84   7   *Literature and Dogma* (1883).
85   23   Psalm 139:7-12.

IX. SHATTERED DREAMS

87   14   Hebrews 11:9.

Page	Line	
88	38	Edward FitzGerald, tr., *Rubáiyát of Omar Khayyám*, Stanza XVI.
89	32	*Ibid.*, Stanza LXIX.
89	35	*Ibid.*, Stanza LXXI.
90	34	Jeremiah 10:19.
93	34	2 Corinthians 11:26.
94	4	Philippians 4:11.
94	17	Philippians 4:7.
94	36	John 14:27.
95	33	Romans 8:28.

X. HOW SHOULD A CHRISTIAN VIEW COMMUNISM?

100	5	Amos 5:24.
100	26	Luke 1:52-53.
100	31	Luke 4:18-19.
104	8	*The Jesus of History* (1917).
105	11	Isaiah 40:4-5.

XI. OUR GOD IS ABLE

106	21	"Hymn of Man" (extract).
111	1	"The Present Crisis" (extract).
111	22	"Life" (extract).
111	36	John 14:27.

XII. ANTIDOTES FOR FEAR

116	16	*Hamlet*, Act III, Scene I.
116	25	From "Courage" in *Society and Solitude* (1870).
118	29	*Discourses.*
124	9	Proverbs 3:19.
124	12	Psalm 8:5.
125	3	Matthew 10:26, 28-31.

XIII. THE ANSWER TO A PERPLEXING QUESTION

132	7	Exodus 14:15.
132	33	Ezekiel 2:1.
136	18	2 Corinthians 5:17 (RSV).
137	2	Revelation 3:20.

XIV. PAUL'S LETTER TO AMERICAN
CHRISTIANS

Page	Line	
139	37	Romans 12:2.
142	6	Galatians 3:28.
142	9	Acts 17:24, 26.
144	21	Romans 8:38-39.
144	32	Matthew 5:11-12.

Also available in Fount Paperbacks

What is Real in Christianity?
DAVID L. EDWARDS

The author strips away the legends from Jesus to show the man who is real, relevant and still fascinating. A clear, confident statement of Christian faith taking account of all criticisms.

The First Christmas
H. J. RICHARDS

Can one really believe in the seventies in such improbable events as the Virgin Birth, the shepherds and the angels, the Magi and the star in the East? Are they just fables? This book suggests that they might be the wrong questions to ask, and may even prevent the reader from arriving at the deeper issues. What these deeper issues are is here explained with clarity, simplicity and honesty.

Wrestling with Christ
LUIGI SANTUCCI

'This is a most unusual book, a prolonged meditation of the life of Christ using many changing literary forms, dialogue, description, addresses to Christ, passages of self-communing. It is written by a Christian passionately concerned that everyone should know Jesus Christ.'   *Catholic Herald*

Journey for a Soul
GEORGE APPLETON

'Wherever you turn in this inexpensive but extraordinarily valuable paperback you will benefit from sharing this man's pilgrimage of the soul.'   *Methodist Recorder*